Welcome to Downtown!
You checked out the following items:

DEEP WOODS
The Story of
ROBERT
FROST

DEEP WOODS

The Story of

ROBERT

FROST

Peggy Caravantes

MORGAN
REYNOLDS

PUBLISHING

Greensboro, North Carolina

WORLD WRITERS

CHARLES DICKENS

JANE AUSTEN

STEPHEN KING

RALPH ELLISON

ROBERT FROST

DEEP WOODS: THE STORY OF ROBERT FROST

Copyright © 2006 by Peggy Caravantes

Library of Congress Cataloging-in-Publication Data

Caravantes, Peggy, 1935-
Deep woods : the story of Robert Frost / Peggy Caravantes.— 1st
    ed. p. cm.
Includes bibliographical references (p.) and index.
ISBN-13: 978-1-931798-92-1 (lib. bdg.)
ISBN-10: 1-931798-92-3 (lib. bdg.)
    1. Frost, Robert, 1874-1963—Juvenile literature. 2. Poets, Ameri-
can—20th century—Biography—Juvenile literature. I. Title.
PS3511.R94Z535 2006
811'.52—dc22

                    2005037514

Printed in the United States of America
First Edition

In loving memory of my mother,
Dorothy Garner Huddleston

Contents

Robert Frost. (Courtesy of Dartmouth College Library.)

one

Seeds of a Poet's Life

Snow fell all night in Washington, DC, covering the ground on the morning of January 20, 1961. Sitting on the platform at the inauguration of John F. Kennedy, the thirty-fifth president of the United States, was an elderly man whose shock of white hair glistened in the bright sun. Despite his heavy black overcoat, he shivered as the ceremony began—a prayer, the national anthem, and the swearing-in of the new vice president, Lyndon B. Johnson.

The eighty-six-year-old man clasped several sheets of paper in one hand, fighting the wind that tried to whip them away. He attended the event at the formal request of President-elect Kennedy, who asked Frost to read one of his poems at the inaugural ceremony. Frost's initial hesitation toward Kennedy's invitation made it difficult for him to feel at ease on the platform. He did not know that Kennedy had initially objected to the suggestion to invite Frost, remarking only half-jokingly, "You know that Frost always steals any show he is part of."

However, Kennedy was a patron of the arts, so he called Frost, suggesting that he write a poem especially for the inauguration. Frost resisted because he had never written for a specific occasion. Kennedy then suggested that Frost's poem "The Gift Outright" be used with a slight change to the last line to present a more optimistic future for the nation. Frost did not like anyone, even the president, manipulating his poetry, so he neither agreed nor disagreed with the suggestion. He did, however, accept the invitation to the inauguration.

Arriving in Washington, DC, Frost had gotten caught up in the spirit of the occasion and decided to write a special piece as an introduction to "The Gift Outright." He typed the forty-two-line "Dedication" on the hotel typewriter. But the print was not very dark. He worried about being able to see the lines in bright sunlight. A Kennedy aide retyped it on a special large-print typewriter that had a new ribbon.

Now Frost sat on the platform, clutching the pages of his offering. His turn at the podium came about at 11 AM with glaring sunlight almost directly overhead. Frost moved unhurriedly to the speaker's stand, where he fumbled with his manuscript pages. In a halting voice, he began to read "Dedication." As he spoke, light struck the pages in a way that prevented his seeing the words. He muttered, "I'm not having a good light here at all. I

DEDICATION

~~Summoning~~
~~Admitting~~ artists to participate

In the august occasions of the state

Seems something for us all to celebrate.

This day is for my cause a day of days,

And his be poetry's old-fashioned praise

Who was the first to think of such a thing.

This tibute verse to be his own I bring

Is about the new order of the ages

That in the Latin of the founding sages

God nodded His approval of as good.

So much those sages knew and understood

(The mighty four of them were Washington,

John Adams, Jefferson, and Madison) -

So much they saw as consecrated seers

They must have seen how in two hundred years

Hours after the inauguration, Kennedy's Secretary of the Interior, Stewart Udall, asked Frost for a copy of the unread poem "Dedication." Frost gave him the very copy he had brought to the ceremony, adding an inscription for Udall in his own hand. (Library of Congress)

can't see in this light." The crowd laughed and applauded as Vice President Johnson rose and walked over to Frost. The vice president used his tall silk hat to shield Frost's manuscript, but Frost brushed him away. In a strong, clear voice, he began reciting from memory "The Gift Outright." As he neared the end of the poem, Frost slowed the last line: "Such as she [America's land] was, such as she *would* become, *has* become, and I—and for this occasion let me change that to—what she *will* become." As the last syllables of the poem died away, the cheers of the crowd showered upon Frost as he turned to thank John F. Kennedy, mistakenly referring to him as Mr. John Finley, a Harvard professor whom Frost knew slightly.

Presidents Dwight Eisenhower and John F. Kennedy shake hands with Frost at the inaugural podium shortly after Frost's reading. (Courtesy of Getty Images.)

If the crowd heard the blunder, they ignored it in their enthusiastic tribute to America's informal poet laureate. Robert Frost had become his own "gift outright" to America's literary world.

Robert Lee Frost entered the world on March 26, 1874, just nine years after the end of the Civil War. Born in a small apartment on Washington Street in San Francisco, California, Robbie was the first child of William Prescott Frost Jr. and Isabelle Moodie Frost. During William Frost's youth in Lawrence, Massachusetts, he gained a reputation as a young man always looking for trouble. His father tried all kinds of discipline and the teenaged William ran away to enlist in the Confederate army because of his strong sympathies for the South. He got as far as Philadelphia before police picked him up and returned him to his parents.

William later applied for admission to West Point but the school turned him down. Embittered, William enrolled at Harvard, his second choice. While there, he completed his assignments quickly so that he could play poker and drink. Despite this lifestyle, William Frost graduated with honors. He decided to leave behind his parents' strict New England standards and head west. San Francisco, with its reputation as the wickedest city in the world, appealed to the headstrong young man. However, he needed money for the trip. He turned down a job offer at the Lawrence mill where his father was foreman and instead took a job as principal and teacher at Lewistown Academy, a private school in Pennsylvania.

He noticed a small ad in the local paper announcing classes in shorthand notation, so William applied to become a student. The instructor was Isabelle Moodie, the only other teacher at Lewistown Academy. The twenty-eight-year-old, called Belle, had come to America from Scotland when she was eight years old. After her father died in a drowning accident at sea, Belle's mother sent the young girl to live with a wealthy aunt and uncle in Ohio.

The handsome Will, with his athletic ability, curly hair, and blue eyes, had not changed from the reckless, impetuous ways of his college days. He cared nothing for religion. Belle, with her dark brown eyes and auburn hair, was shy, reserved, hesitant, and deeply religious. Despite these differences, within five months Will won Belle's heart. They married on March 18, 1873, and both quit their jobs at the end of the school term.

Will traveled ahead by Union Pacific Railroad to California, leaving Belle with her Ohio relatives. After finding a newspaper job and a place to live, Will sent for his wife.

At that time San Francisco had rolled right out of the Gold Rush into a silver-mining boom. Treasure hunters arrived in unending numbers that peaked at the time Will and Belle settled in the city. In addition, over 60,000 immigrants, mostly from China, arrived by ship each year. Will Frost thrived in the environment. He worked first for the *Daily Evening Bulletin* and later for the *Daily Evening Post*. Like other editors and reporters who

By the mid-1870s, the once-small settlement of San Francisco had become a booming port bursting with fortune-seekers, immigrant laborers, and frontiersmen. (Library of Congress)

assured him it was a common practice, William Frost purchased a revolver as a means of self-defense. Because of the prevalence of weapons in San Francisco, the doctor who delivered Robbie showed little surprise when William pulled a gun and threatened to shoot the physician if anything happened to the baby or its mother. Upon the safe arrival of the child, Will chose the boy's name to reflect his sympathy with the South in the Civil War and his admiration for its top general, Robert E. Lee.

After Robbie's birth, Will became involved in politics, enthusiastically supporting his preferred candidates and unsuccessfully running for several minor offices himself. But Will Frost also continued the pattern he had begun in college—gambling and drinking. The more he drank, the more Belle retreated into her religion. She had joined the Swedenborgian Church, a mystical religion established by the Swedish philosopher Emanuel Swedenborg.

By the time Robbie was two years old, relations between Will and Belle were even more strained. About this time, Belle realized that she was pregnant with their second child. Fearful of her husband's violence when he was drinking, Belle took her young son east to visit her in-laws in the summer of 1876. She had never met them. The older Frosts did not receive their daughter-in-law with much warmth. They saw no reason that a pregnant woman should leave her husband and travel cross-country alone. Belle did not tell them about their son's drinking.

Will wrote to Belle, begging her to return to San Francisco. He promised to change his ways. Before Belle could decide what she wanted to do, she gave birth on June 25, 1876, to a daughter whom she named Jeanie Florence Frost. Since her in-laws did not seem to want her to extend her visit, Belle left as soon as she could travel. She went to visit an old friend on her parents' farm in Greenfield. The entire family warmly welcomed Belle and her two children.

Throughout the summer Belle and Will wrote letters to each other. Will told Belle that his health was poor because he had participated in a six-day footrace, trying to beat the local champion. Worried, Belle returned to San Francisco in September. When Belle arrived, she found her husband in the hospital. He was coughing up

Robbie Frost's father, the handsome but troubled William Prescott Frost Jr. (Courtesy of Dartmouth College Library.)

blood, a symptom of one of the dreaded diseases of the day, tuberculosis.

Despite his health problems, Will refused to accept the seriousness of his condition. Belle retreated further into religion. Thinking he could get enough money to go to Hawaii, where he believed he could be cured, Will invested most of his weekly salary in silver-mining shares. Their finances strained, the family moved frequently to different hotel rooms and apartments whenever they could not pay their rent.

When Robbie was five years old, the Frosts sent him to a private kindergarten run by a Russian woman, Madame Zitska. To reach her house, halfway across town, Robbie had to ride in a horse-drawn bus. On his first return trip home, a new driver had difficulty finding Robbie's house. Robbie panicked, thinking he would never again see his mother. He suffered, or at least complained of suffering, terrible stomach cramps, and repeated his protests whenever he had to go to school. Eventually, Belle let him stay home.

In the autumn of 1860, Belle tried again to get her son to attend school. When he made the usual stomachache complaint to avoid going to first grade, Belle told the boy that he could stay home until he felt well enough to return to school. Robbie never reached that point, and his mother began teaching him reading, writing, and arithmetic at home. Robbie was not a strong student in reading or arithmetic, but he excelled in writing. He quickly learned to form the letters of the alphabet and to write words. His mother gave him a copybook in which Robbie carefully copied sentences. When he made a mistake in his lettering, he went into a rage, ripping the sheet from his copybook and crushing it in his hand.

Robbie made enough progress to attend second grade in public school the following year. This time he went until February, when the teacher punished him, hitting his hand because he had misbehaved. The next morning he complained of stomach cramps, beginning a pattern that kept him out of school the rest of the year. The cycle repeated the following year.

Belle knew that she overindulged her son, but she

hoped that her kindness offset Robbie's exposure to the drunken rages of his father. Will Frost was not at the house very often, but when he was home, he was a strict disciplinarian. Will came home drunk one afternoon while Robbie and a friend sat on the living-room carpet building a ship model from little pieces of wood. When Will saw glue and wood chips scattered across the floor, he walked over to the boys, lifted his foot, and stomped on the ship. Then with the back of his hand, he struck Robbie several times.

To get the children out of the house on the weekends, Belle took them for long walks all over San Francisco. They climbed the many hills and looked with awe at the elaborate Victorian-style Nob Hill mansions built by wealthy men who had accumulated great fortunes from gold and silver. They went to the waterfront to watch the boats and feed the seagulls.

Will did not usually accompany the family on these outings. But sometimes he took Robbie to the beach while he practiced long-distance swimming. Despite his declining health, Will pushed himself to test his body's limits. One day after work, he and Robbie walked to the shore. Will left the young boy on the beach to watch his clothes, towel, and whiskey bottle while he swam a half-mile through cold, choppy waters. Each time Will reached a buoy marker, he climbed up on it and waved at Robbie. The boy admired his father's athletic ability, but each time Will disappeared beneath a wave, Robbie panicked.

As Robbie grew older, he explored the neighborhood

Jeanie and Robbie Frost, 1876. (Courtesy of Dartmouth College Library.)

alone. He encountered a gang of boys that roamed the streets and engaged in petty thievery. Robbie wanted to join the Washington Street gang but had to go through a two-part initiation—fighting one of the gang's members and stealing. The gang's leader, Seth Balsa, asked Robbie if he could fight. Although he had never fought, Robbie wanted to impress the older boy. He bragged that he could fight two boys at once. Seth picked two boys from the gang, and they gave Robbie a licking.

Hearing that her son had been fighting horrified Belle, but Will saw it as a sign of Robbie's toughness. Despite losing the fight, Robbie gained the gang members' admiration for his courage. They invited him into the gang, but one test remained. The gang leader wanted a new pair of wheels for his four-wheel wagon on which he coasted down the San Francisco hills. Balsa had seen a pair of wheels in a basement on Leavenworth Street. However, he could not fit through the cellar's window. Flattered to do something for the gang's leader, Robbie went with him to the house. They crawled under the porch where Balsa pried the window open. Robbie went feet-first through the window and landed on the cellar floor. With some matches provided by Balsa, Robbie located the wheels and handed them out the window.

Several boys in the gang sold newspapers on the downtown streets of San Francisco. Ten-year-old Robbie, who still did not attend school, asked his parents' permission to become a paperboy. They finally agreed, but when Robbie discovered how little money he made for long hours standing on the street, he quit.

To offset Robbie's lack of formal education, his mother read to him and his sister Jeanie from a wide variety of

Young Robbie Frost's favorite story, At the Back of the North Wind, *describes the fanciful adventures of Diamond, a boy who is beckoned by a beautiful woman with flashing eyes and streaming black hair to fly through the dark on secret excursions requiring strength, bravery, and truth.*

sources: *Tom Brown's Schooldays, The Last of the Mohicans, The Mysterious Island,* and Robbie's favorite, *At the Back of the North Wind.* Belle included stories about such Scottish heroes as Sir William Wallace and Robert the Bruce (King Robert I) as well as the poetry of Robert Burns. She also made sure that the children received religious training. As a child Robbie was baptized in a Presbyterian church, attended Sunday school at a Unitarian church, and then worshipped with the Swedenborgians. In later years, he told a friend, "All this baptizing and church and Sunday school going may have had a bad effect on me. I did so much of it when young that I never felt any call to continue it later in life."

Will Frost earned $2,000 a year, considered a good salary in 1884. But his speculation in the silver mines, along with drinking and gambling, drained the family income. Will decided to run for city tax collector, a job that would pay more than his newspaper salary. In June, he resigned from his job as city editor, leaving the family with no income. Much to his surprise, Will lost the election and had to seek another job. He did find a position with the *Daily Report*, but by then the tuberculosis was taking its toll.

When Will spit up blood, Belle told the children that he had the flu. Will tried all kinds of remedies, hoping for a miraculous cure. Once he took Robbie with him to the slaughterhouse where he drank cup after cup of fresh blood from a steer's slit throat. By the spring of 1885, Will knew he was dying. He wrote to his parents in Lawrence, Massachusetts, to ask them to take care of his wife and children. He did not tell them the truth about his disease. He also did not tell his wife that he had failed to keep up the payments on his $20,000 life insurance policy.

On the morning of May 5, 1885, Belle sent the children outside to play. When they later looked toward their front door, they saw a piece of black crepe—a sign of death. William Prescott Frost Jr. had died at the age of thirty-four. The shock to eleven-year-old Robbie was so great that he later said, "I never spoke of my father for years after he went: I couldn't." After Belle paid funeral expenses and took care of the remaining bills, she had eight dollars left. Will had wanted to be buried in New England, but Belle had no money to transport his body or to pay for train tickets for her and the children.

Belle did not want to be dependent on her in-laws, but she had little choice. The elder Frosts sent enough money to bring all of them, including their son's body, to Massachusetts. The family traveled with the coffin across the bay to Oakland, where they boarded a train to go east. In later years, Frost described that train ride as "the *longest, loneliest* train ride" of his life.

After the funeral, Belle wished that she could return to her friends and her church in San Francisco, but she had no way to get money for the trip. Even if she found transportation, she was not sure that she could support herself and her children in California. She had to remain with her in-laws, at least for a while. As Belle looked for a way that her family could leave, Benjamin and Sarah Frost Messer, an uncle and aunt of Will's, invited them to New Hampshire to help with berry picking and canning. On the small farm, Robbie and Jeanie enjoyed wagon rides through landscapes they had never seen in California—forests of tall elm trees, stretches of green grass, farmlands, and orchards.

In the fall, the Messers invited them to stay longer. That way the children could attend the local public school. However, both Robbie and Jeanie immediately complained. Robbie did not like the teachers, and Jeanie did not like anything about the school. Since Belle did not have any special qualifications as a teacher—no college degree and no teaching certificate—finding a job was not easy. Another uncle and aunt, Elihu and Lucy Frost Colcord, allowed the itinerant family to stay with them for a while. Unfortunately, the couple soon decided that they did not want so many people in their house. When Belle finally found a teaching job in Salem Depot, the Colcords loaned her enough money to rent a shabby two-room apartment. Belle earned $400 a year and taught the students in grades five to eight. Both Robbie and Jeanie were in her class.

From the beginning, Belle had difficulty controlling her classes. Despite the discipline problems, Belle used some original teaching methods. She seated children according to their ability with the lower-performing students sitting in the front near her desk. In contrast to the rote memorization methods popular at the time, Belle instructed her students individually according to each one's needs. She read aloud to her classes every day and recognized the students who pursued literature outside the class.

Belle received both praise and criticism for encouraging the brighter eighth graders to continue their education by attending high school. Many of the parents praised her different outlook. An equal number wanted to see her fired for meddling with the common practice of students going to work after the eighth grade.

School bored Robbie, and he spent most of his time whittling wooden figures behind a large, propped-up geography book. His mother chose to ignore the wood shavings that piled up on the floor under his desk. That year Robbie discovered that he liked baseball, especially pitching. As his passion for the sport grew, Belle tried to use this interest to get Robbie to read. However, she was unsuccessful. In fact, Robbie did not read a book by himself until he was fourteen.

During this time, Robbie became best friends with Charley Peabody. Charley's dad taught them how to track and trap, and how to skin a rabbit. With the Peabody boys, Robbie climbed birches and rode them to the ground. The Peabodys introduced Robbie to nature, which would later become so important to his writing. Belle decided, however, that Robbie should spend less time in the woods and use the summer to help with the family's always-unstable finances. When Robbie found a job at the Salem shoe factory at a salary of $1.50 a day, his mother acknowledged he was growing up by starting to call him Rob.

two

"The Self Seeker"

Rob's job at the factory required him to hammer three nails into each leather shoe. Because of the good job he did, he was soon promoted to a position using a machine to cut leather patterns. From the beginning Rob hated it. Another boy had lost a finger on the same machine when he did not get his hand clear of the blade quickly enough. Rob wanted to quit but did not want anyone to know he was afraid, so he lied to his mother that the men who worked around him cursed all the time. The religious Belle demanded that Rob leave the job immediately.

Belle returned to her teaching job in Salem Depot that fall. However, she was not well. She was extremely thin, and her dark hair had become dry and untidy. More and more she ignored student misbehavior. Some of her students complained to their parents, who went to the

Belle Moodie Frost. (Courtesy of Dartmouth College Library.)

school board. The town was divided over whether to fire her. At the same time that Belle faced this professional dilemma, she confided to a friend she was worried about her children. Jeanie seemed withdrawn, wanting to do nothing but read. Rob had apparently inherited his father's hot temper and stubbornness. He showed little ambition. Belle worried that her indulgence had led to his laziness.

Since Rob wanted to qualify for the high school baseball team when he became a freshman at Lawrence High School, he began to study for the first time in his life. He had read his first book when his employer's wife told him about *The Scottish Chiefs*, a historical novel. She told Rob just enough of the plot to pique his interest. When she let him borrow her copy, he read the entire book without stopping. In one of his textbooks, he read some poems that he liked so much that he memorized them. When Rob took the high school entrance exams, he barely passed the arithmetic test. However, his scores on the other subjects were high enough to qualify him. His sister Jeanie also met the requirements to attend.

In the fall of 1888, brother and sister began their daily seven-mile commute by train from Salem Depot to Lawrence, Massachusetts. As he listened to other students talking, Rob learned that his mother continued to have trouble disciplining her students. The school board decided not to fire her, but many unhappy parents withdrew their students from the school. By the end of the year, Belle tired of the struggle and decided to leave Salem Depot. Upon hearing the news, Rob vowed, "You wait. Some day, I'll come back to Salem Depot—and show them."

At the high school, Rob chose the classical curriculum

to prepare himself for college. During his sophomore year, he became friends with Carl Burell, who was ten years older. Burell had left school without graduating and now worked as a janitor and handyman at the school while trying to complete his education. He had an unusual intellectual curiosity that appealed to Rob. Burell loaned books to Rob and was the first to introduce him to botany and astronomy, two interests that Rob Frost held throughout his lifetime. While reading *Our Place Among Infinities* by the British astronomer Richard Anthony Proctor, Rob studied the conflict between science and religion. A few lines brought him reassurance as a teenager and throughout most of his adult life: "In a word, our faith must not be hampered by scientific doubts, our science must not be hampered by religious scruples."

His English class further kindled for Rob's interest in poetry. One teacher wrote William Collins's "How Sleep the Brave" on the blackboard, a poem from the 1700s commemorating English soldiers fallen in battle. The rhythm and diction of the piece excited Rob. He discovered poetry by Percy Bysshe Shelley, John Keats, Edgar Allan Poe, and Matthew Arnold. Soon, Rob wanted to write poetry as well as to read it. One night, while walking to his grandmother's house, where he sometimes stayed, Rob thought back on the day's reading from William Prescott's *History of the Conquest of Mexico*. The passage described the night when the Aztecs retreated across the causeway over Lake Tezcuco from the island city of Tenochtitlan. A poem began to form.

He swung his textbooks wrapped together with a leather strap as a metronome so that he could get the rhythm he wanted. He later recalled, "I had never written a poem before, and as I walked, it appeared like a revelation, and I became so taken by it that I was late at my grandmother's." At her house, he wrote twenty-five stanzas without stopping. Rob titled the poem "La Noche Triste," meaning "the sad night." He believed that this incident prophesied his future as a great poet.

The next morning Rob left the poem on the desk of Ernest Jewell, a senior and the editor of the high school's *Bulletin*. Jewell published it on the front page of the school paper in April 1890.

By the time Frost became a senior, he was editor of that same school paper. He also played on the varsity football team. One of the staff members on the *Bulletin* wrote, "No one would think the man who played football on the right end was the same person who sits with spectacles astride his nose in the Chief Editor's Chair. Keep up the good work, Bobby."

Despite her intelligence, Jeanie struggled with school due to insomnia and depression. In December of her senior year, she dropped out. Rob worried about his sister and his own experiences with anxiety and depression. Whenever these feelings came over him, he threw himself into frantic activity, a pattern that lasted the rest of his life.

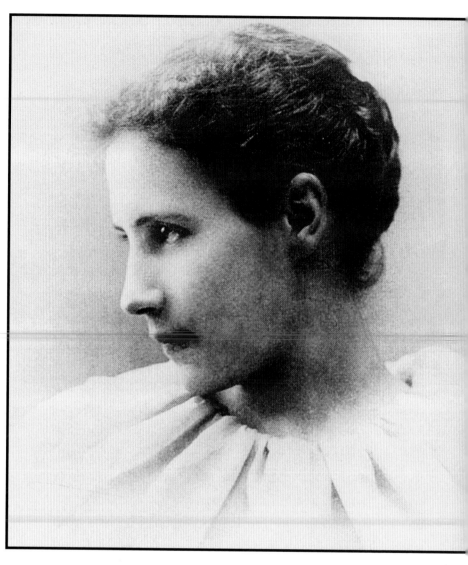

Elinor Miriam White in 1892, the year she and Frost graduated from Lawrence High School as co-valedictorians. (Courtesy of Dartmouth College Library.)

Rob and another student, Elinor Miriam White, alternated being the top student in their class. Elinor pursued a general course of study rather than the college preparatory route Rob followed. Though they were in the same class, Elinor was one-and-a-half-years older than Rob.

A lingering illness had held her back in school. As they vied for valedictorian honors, the two became friends. They had much in common—a love of poetry, family financial problems, a sister who had dropped out of school, and the feeling of not belonging in Lawrence. By midway through their senior year, Rob began courting Elinor. As the school year drew to a close, the principal named Rob and Elinor co-valedictorians. At graduation, Rob also received the Hood Prize, a small gold medal for general excellence and conduct in his four years in high school.

Rob proposed to Elinor in June 1892. They secretly held a private, unofficial marriage ceremony but told no one else about it. Eighteen-year-old Frost was bound for Dartmouth College in Hanover, New Hampshire, while Elinor planned to attend St. Lawrence University in Canton, New York.

Founded in 1769, Dartmouth College is the ninth-oldest college in the United States. (Library of Congress)

At Dartmouth, Frost embraced college life, and his socializing earned him an invitation to join a fraternity, Theta Delta Chi. He initially declined membership, stating that he could not afford the initiation fee, but a senior member paid the fee for him.

Despite the fun, Frost missed Elinor. He took long, solitary walks to think about her. He worried because her letters sounded as if she were enjoying college life and making new friends. She did not seem to miss him, and Frost resented her not being as miserable as he was. Frost hated having to meet deadlines for his college courses, and by the end of the first semester, he was ready to quit. Upon learning that the eighth-grade boys in Belle's new school in Methuen, Massachusetts, were giving her a hard time, Frost decided to replace his mother as the boys' teacher.

Without telling anyone, Frost left Dartmouth. In later years he explained, "I was glad to seize the excuse (to myself) that my mother needed me in her school to take care of some big, brutal boys she could not manage." Although Frost worried about his mother's reaction to his leaving college, he cared nothing for what others thought. His plan was to go to the school board and appeal to them to let him assume his mother's teaching duties. Frost told the Reverend Charles H. Oliphant, school board president, that dealing with the unruly boys was having a negative effect on Belle's health.

Although he was a family friend, Reverend Oliphant had doubts about Frost's ability to teach and manage the boys. Frost persisted, showing signs of the strong-willed nature that characterized him in adulthood. Oliphant met with the school board and first requested that they transfer Belle Frost to a primary grade, where the discipline would not be so challenging. After accepting that suggestion, the board also approved Frost's appointment as the eighth-grade teacher.

While he waited to hear the board's decision, Frost purchased several rattan canes from the local hardware store. On his first day to meet the class, Frost told them exactly why he was there. He scolded the boys for their behavior and told them he planned to get even. Several of the boys were as big as he was, so Frost decided to make an example of a middle-sized boy who misbehaved. Watching for his opportunity, Frost took the boy into the hall to lash him with the rattan. The rest of the class rebelled, yelling and misbehaving. Frost realized that to gain control, he must take on the bigger class leaders.

However, the larger boys did not easily surrender to the whippings. The more they resisted, the angrier Frost became. He thrashed them so violently that one boy pulled out a knife. Frost managed to twist the boy's wrist until he dropped the knife. After school that day, Frost went to talk to Reverend Oliphant. He explained that the boys had become so unruly that he had used stronger physical punishment than he had intended. He showed the school board chairman the knife as proof of the boys' rowdiness. By the time some of the boys' parents came to complain, the school board had already decided to support Frost in bringing the boys under control.

The daily whippings took their toll on Frost, who resigned at the end of the term in March. Although he had planned to stay until the end of the school year in June, he told himself that he had obtained revenge for the way the boys had treated his mother. The disruptive students bragged that they had run their teacher off. With no other job in sight, Frost became depressed, a condition that periodically overwhelmed him for the rest of his life.

When his sweetheart Elinor made a trip home because her older sister Ada was ill, Frost tried to persuade her to stay. He wanted to announce their "secret" marriage, promising he would support them with his poetry, but Elinor was skeptical. They argued, and finally Elinor agreed to stay through the summer. Frost, Elinor, her sister, and her mother took up residence in a cottage, where the Whites hoped Ada's health would improve.

When the three women left that fall, Frost stayed on alone. The quiet and solitude agreed with him, and he wrote "Bereft," a poem that went unpublished until 1927. In it he found hints of his poetic voice as he reflected on his feeling of loneliness with only God for comfort and company:

> Word I was in the house alone
> Somehow must have gotten abroad,
> Word I was in my life alone,
> Word I had no one left but God.

Robert Frost in 1892. (Courtesy of Dartmouth College Library.)

News of his paternal grandmother's death added to
Frost's melancholy. He knew that he would miss her. She
had always approved of her grandson's artistic ambitions

and encouraged Frost's grandfather to support him financially.

In September, Frost moved back into the tiny two-room apartment with his mother and sister. With no plans and no income, he answered an ad in a Boston newspaper to manage the performances of a Shakespearean actor. When he met with the actor, Frost pretended to have theater experience. However, seeing how badly the actor performed, Frost changed his mind about taking the job.

Desperate for cash, Frost finally got a low-level job with the Arlington Woolen Mill. He replaced carbon-pencil filaments of the popular arc lamps. He had just started this job when the school board let Belle go because she had continued to have problems even after the move to a primary school. The total family income was Frost's salary of eight dollars per week. One day he arrived at the mill just as the huge gates swung closed. He was locked out, and his pay would be docked for the time he missed until the gates opened again.

Frost took a train to Salem Depot, where he approached a member of the school board about a job. The board hired him as a substitute teacher in a small school. Though it did not increase his income, he enjoyed the shorter hours and working with children in grades one to six. He still dreamed about becoming a poet but shared that goal with no one.

At night, after his mother and sister were in bed, Frost locked himself in the kitchen to work on his poems. However, his sister Jeanie often disturbed his creativity by pounding on the door most of the night. Jeanie's mental state concerned Frost, who knew he had his own dark tendencies. He was doing everything he could to ward them off. Writing poetry became for him what he later called "a momentary stay against confusion."

One of the poems—"My Butterfly: An Elegy"—was based on an experience at Dartmouth, where he found a fragile butterfly wing among some dead leaves. He felt good about the poem and believed that he had made progress in his technique. In 1894, he submitted it to Reverend William Hayes Ward, the editor of *The Independent*, a respectable national journal. A few days later Frost received a check for $15 (over $300 in today's currency), along with praise for the poem and questions about himself. Frost told the editor that he had deter-

Reverend William Hayes Ward, editor of the esteemed weekly journal, The Independent. (Library of Congress)

mined to become a poet and nothing would distract him.

While Frost was still celebrating the sale, he received the poem in the mail with revision suggestions made by the editor's sister, Susan Hayes Ward. Frost did not like criticism of his work. After several revisions, he became despondent and wanted to throw the poem away. However, Susan Ward had experience working with writers and she kept pushing Frost to get the poem ready for fall publication.

Frost showed his poems to friends, including the Reverend William E. Wolcott, who offered to serve as an editing adviser to Frost. However, in looking through other poems, he did not find anything as good "My Butterfly." Wolcott found Frost's poetry lacking in a lyrical quality and suggested that Frost try a more formal, dignified tone, because the way it was written reminded him too much of someone speaking.

Wolcott's criticism threw light on something with which Frost had been struggling. Although he had not yet articulated it, Frost realized that he did want to make his poetry sound like actual speech. Frost later told a friend, "I'm sure the old gentleman didn't have the slightest idea he was having any effect on a very stubborn youngster who thought he knew what he knew. But something he said actually changed the whole course of my writing. It all became purposeful." Frost realized that a good poem could sound like speech and that all the lines and sentences should clearly convey a tone of voice that could root poetry deep in the human experience. From then on, he decided that he would try harder to make his poetry sound like true oral expression.

When Elinor came home for summer vacation, Frost again pushed her to make their private marriage public. The only concession that Elinor made was to take more courses so that she could graduate a year early. If Frost could support them at that time, she promised to marry him.

In the spring of 1894, Frost taught a class for one semester at Salem Depot. He did not work the rest of that year. Concerned about Frost's drifting from job to job, his paternal grandfather offered to finance him for a year while Frost tried to establish himself as a poet. However, if at the end of the year he had not succeeded, he would have to give up the idea of becoming a poet and find a job. Frost refused his grandfather's offer because he believed it would take at least twenty years to become the kind of poet he planned to be.

Jealous of Elinor's life and friends at college, Frost took five love poems, including "My Butterfly," to a Lawrence print shop. He paid to have the poems printed on antique paper and bound in leather. He had just two copies made of the volume he called "Twilight." He took a train to Elinor's university, where he presented her with one copy. She did not receive his surprise visit with much enthusiasm and seemed unimpressed by the volume of poetry. Frost grew so despondent that he did not wait for the return train. He started walking along the tracks, tearing his book of poetry into shreds.

Desperate to get Elinor's attention so that she would

understand how much he loved her, Frost briefly considered suicide but decided instead to disappear for a while. He packed a bag and left home without even telling his mother. He headed for the twenty-mile-long Great Dismal Swamp along the eastern North Carolina-Virginia border. Its bogs, quicksand, and thick trees and vines matched his dark mood. When he arrived, Frost walked alone ten miles into the interior of the swamp. A friend later remarked, "I often think how hard that would have been for Robert. He was always terrified of the dark. . . . It was a thing left over from his boyhood."

As he trudged along, not wanting to go on living without Elinor, Frost met a group of duck hunters. They invited Frost to join them, and he rode on their boat back to Elizabeth City, North Carolina. Frost entertained several offers of work but felt too homesick to stick around. He hopped a train that ultimately got him to Washington, DC. From there, he managed to make his way to a town just outside of Baltimore. Frost got a job as a handyman for a local grocer in exchange for room and board until he worked up the nerve to wire his mother for the money to buy a train ticket home. He later told one of his biographers: "I suppose it was all nothing but my young way of having the blues."

Still, the ploy worked. Elinor agreed to marry him as soon as she graduated. Meanwhile, Belle Frost decided to open a private school with her daughter Jeanie and soon-to-be daughter-in-law as teachers. She found a couple of offices that she converted to classrooms. Frost briefly returned to his job at the Salem District School #9. When Belle became ill that spring, Frost resigned from Salem. He assumed his mother's teaching duties at her new school, but life was far from perfect. Frost found stress in every area of his life, from teaching upper-level courses to living with his mother and sister.

The stress blocked his creative flow, even as *The Independent* had shown an interest in seeing more of Frost's poems. All inspiration seemed to have left him. He began to suffer severe stomach pains and night sweats. Doctors attributed his problems to nervous tension. Despite these hardships, Frost could take heart in his ability to provide for Elinor and his family through teaching.

Not everyone believed in Frost. Elinor's father did not approve of her marriage and refused to give her a church wedding. One of the classrooms in Belle's school became the site of Robert and Elinor's wedding on December 19, 1895. A family friend, Reverend John A. Hayes, a Swedenborgian minister, performed the ceremony. Twenty-one-year-old Robert and twenty-three-year-old Elinor postponed their honeymoon until the summer. The couple moved in with Belle and Jeanie.

Frost had achieved his years-long goal of marrying his true love. By doing so, he had gained some semblance of an adult life, and with that came responsibility. Now, his desire, his need, to write poems weighed heaviest on his soul.

three

A Poet's Will

The following June, his friend Carl Burell helped Frost find a small country cottage where he could take Elinor for their delayed honeymoon. Burell continued to spur Frost's interest in botany by showing him the intricacies of nature's details. Frost began reading Burell's botany books and learned quickly, becoming a keen observer of nature. For a while Elinor accompanied Frost on his nature walks but gradually stopped because she was pregnant, despite her doctor's warning that her weak heart might not withstand the stress of childbearing.

Blond, blue-eyed Elliott Frost arrived on September 25, 1896. He fascinated Elinor, who spent so much time with the baby that Frost became jealous. However, he took the responsibilities of fatherhood seriously and started to look for a better-paying job. When Frost told his grandfather that he would like to teach high school Greek and Latin, the elder Frost agreed to pay the tuition to Harvard so that Frost could prepare himself. After passing the entrance exams, Frost, five years older than most of the freshmen, entered Harvard as a special student. Elinor, Elliott, and Elinor's mother, who stayed with the family temporarily, joined him in a small apartment in Cambridge.

The summer after Frost completed his first year at Harvard, Elinor became pregnant again. She did not return to Cambridge with him for the fall semester but stayed with her parents in Lawrence. Frost did well enough in the first semester of his second year to win a prize for excellence in classical studies. Although proud of the award, Frost already knew that he would not stay at Harvard. His marriage was suffering the strain of distance, and his mother and sister both needed more support. The mental depression that so often overcame him led to physical ailments—headaches, night sweats and breathing problems. He feared getting tuberculosis, his father's killer, and began to imagine his own impending death.

Frost knew he needed to leave Harvard, and the news that Elinor's pregnancy was affecting her health gave him the excuse he needed. In March 1899, he returned to Lawrence, though his headaches and fatigue did not go away. In later years, he told some students at Harvard, "They could not make a student of me here, but they gave it their best."

Before Frost left, the dean promised him a good recommendation. Frost still had no degree, but he took with him a strong knowledge of Greek and Latin, American poetry, and philosophy.

Doctors warned him against a sedentary lifestyle and recommended farming to improve his health. The Frosts' second child, Lesley, was born on April 28, 1899, and in May, Frost rented a place in Methuen, Massachusetts, with plans to operate a poultry farm. A veterinarian friend had a prosperous operation nearby and agreed to advise Frost. As usual, the poet needed money to get started and went again to his grandfather. This time the older man treated the loan as a true business deal and made Frost sign papers and agree to pay interest.

Frost built shelters for the incubators and followed his friend's advice exactly. The change in lifestyle brought about improvement in his health. Then he learned that doctors had diagnosed advanced cancer in his mother. Belle came to live with Frost and Elinor while his sister Jeanie went to stay with friends in Lawrence.

The poultry farm prospered, and for a short while, the Frosts enjoyed their most stable financial time. In July 1900, though, their son Elliott became ill with severe digestive problems and high fever. Since Belle's doctor was visiting her that day, he agreed to examine Elliott. He gave the child some medicine, but Elliott's condition continued to worsen. The Frosts called their own doctor, who was angry that he had not been contacted sooner. He told the Frosts, "This is *cholera infantum* [severe infant intestinal disease]. It's too late, now, for me to do anything. The child will be dead before morning." Little Elliot died at 4:00 AM on July 8.

Frost believed that he had murdered his own son by not calling the doctor sooner. Elinor sank into a deep depression that led her to doubt the existence of God. She would remain an atheist the rest of her life. The Frosts still had to face other challenges: Lesley was a sickly child and Belle's condition had worsened. Frost had to take care of the farm, despite the return of his stress-related stomach pains and night sweats. He worried again that he might have tuberculosis. In August he accepted the suggestion of his mother's doctor to move Belle to Alexander Sanitarium in New Hampshire. Jeanie did not agree with the decision and criticized her brother, claiming he just wanted to get rid of their mother.

Things were going from bad to worse. By this time the rent on their house was overdue by several months. The house's condition shocked the landlord when she came to collect the payments. She told the Frosts that they had to move out by the end of the month. Elinor's mother found them a thirty-acre farm in Derry, New Hampshire, just north of Salem and about twelve miles from Lawrence. The property had an almost-new farmhouse, a barn, and an apple orchard.

Once again the Frosts looked to Robert's grandfather for help. Elinor herself asked him for help in buying the farm. He sent Elihu Colcord, Frost's uncle, with whom he had once lived, to see if the farm was worth the $1,700 price. Colcord gave a positive report. In addition to the buildings, he found a large field of maple, oak, beech and alders. A brook ran across the property, and berries and a vegetable garden could provide food for the family. Grandfather Frost bought the farm and allowed Robert to rent it from him.

The Frosts moved to the Derry farm in October 1900 and stayed for the next eleven years. This move began the most important phase of Frost's life. Besides gaining a stability he had rarely known, Frost came into contact with material that he drew on for beautiful imagery in a lifetime of writing poetry. In later years, Frost said, "It all started in Derry, the whole thing." During the day Frost worked the farm; at night he wrote poetry in the kitchen.

On November 2, Belle Frost died at the age of fifty-six; the family buried her in Lawrence. Frost went into a period of depression that lasted until the spring. In July, his grandfather, William Frost, died, leaving his grandson a $500 annuity and use of the Derry farm rent-free for ten years. At the end of that time, the annuity would increase to $800 and ownership of the farm would pass to Frost. He had hoped his grandson would finally dedicate himself to providing a good home for his wife and growing family.

The Frosts welcomed a son, Carol, in 1902, a daughter, Irma, in 1903, and another daughter, Marjorie, in 1905. Frost enjoyed spending time with his children—taking nature walks, raking leaves to build a bonfire, and

The four Frost children play in the front yard of the farmhouse in Derry, New Hampshire, 1908. (Courtesy of Dartmouth College Library.)

looking at the moon and stars. However, like the New Englanders in his poems, Frost remained reserved and undemonstrative with his children. He rarely hugged or kissed them. He and Elinor had a difficult, often fractious relationship.

Once, when Robert and Elinor's arguing had peaked, Robert went to their daughter Lesley's room in the middle of the night, woke her up, and then took her barefoot through the cold, dark house. When they reached the kitchen, a single light revealed Elinor sitting at the table, holding her head and sobbing. Frost pointed a pistol at himself and then at Elinor. He shouted to Lesley,

"Take your choice. Before morning, one of us will be dead!" The terrified child stood still, trembling, unable to choose one parent over the other. Elinor rose from the table, wrapped her arms around Lesley, and led her back to her bed. The ugly incident remained in Lesley's mind, and she held it against her father into adulthood.

At times like this, Frost despaired of his worth as a father and husband. When such periods of depression overcame him, he walked in the woods until he was exhausted. He had put little time into the poultry farm since receiving his grandfather's annuity and the business suffered. Finances again became strained. Finally, he decided "to do what I hated to do—and what I didn't want to do, what I had never liked to do—go back to the drudgery of teaching."

With the help of friends, Frost obtained a part-time position in March 1906 at Pinkerton Academy, about two miles north of his farm. He taught two classes of sophomore English for a salary of $285 for the term. Frost went out of his way to make the classes interesting. He placed a heavy emphasis on craft, leading discussions on the art of writing. The next fall he began a full-time schedule that included teaching all of the school's English classes, tutoring in other subjects, coaching the debate team, advising the school paper, and helping with athletics. His salary was $1,000 per year.

In the spring of 1907, at thirty-three years old, Frost developed a severe case of pneumonia and had to stay home during March and April. Elinor tried to care for

Pinkerton Academy in Derry, New Hampshire, where Frost taught from 1905 to 1911.
(Library of Congress)

him, but she was pregnant for the sixth time. She became ill and had to move into town, where a nurse could care for her. She stayed there until June 18 when Elinor Bettina was born. The baby died three days later. Although Elinor accepted the child's death as one of life's tragedies, Frost blamed himself for having overworked his wife. Both Robert and Elinor realized that they needed a change. In July and August, the entire family went to Bethlehem, New Hampshire, a small village in the White Mountains.

That fall, Frost began the new semester with enthusiasm and with innovative teaching techniques that some of his fellow faculty members criticized. He made his students memorize poetry and read aloud in class. To bring the literature to life, he produced five plays each year. He believed that students must be encouraged to rely on their own personal experiences rather than to absorb information only from books and their teachers. He wanted them to think independently and to develop ideas of their own. He believed that students should be active participants in their education rather than passive recipients. His classroom style was casual with discussion taking the place of lecture. Frost gave exams but seldom graded them.

Despite some of his fellow teachers' opinions, Frost impressed the state superintendent of instruction, who invited Frost to address a New Hampshire teachers' convention on methods of teaching English. Frost was so nervous about speaking publicly to anyone except his students that he broke out in cold sweats and suffered stomach cramps. Nevertheless, he delivered the speech, which was well received by the other teachers.

When Pinkerton's principal, Ernest Silver, resigned to take a similar position at New Hampshire State Normal School, a teachers' college in Plymouth, he invited Frost to go with him. There were no English openings, but Silver convinced Frost that he could teach psychology and the history of education, at least temporarily. Frost agreed, but with the condition that he would only teach the subjects for one year.

Frost enjoyed his time at New Hampshire State. When he started playing tennis to get some exercise, one of his opponents was a twenty-two-year-old high school teacher, Sidney Cox. As they took long walks together and discussed literature, they began a friendship that lasted a lifetime. Another benefit of being at the college was that it gave Frost the opportunity to do what he had desired for some time—sell the Derry farm, which had transferred to his name in 1911. But he could not find a buyer. Because he had neglected the farm during his years at Pinkerton Academy and had failed to make several monthly payments, he netted only $1,200 when he sold the mortgage to the bank.

By the spring of 1912, Frost had passed his thirty-eighth birthday but had still not fulfilled his dream of publishing a book of poetry. He had been writing when time and his mental health afforded it, sometimes steadily, at other times sporadically. But he realized that if he continued teaching, its demands would prevent his reaching that goal of publishing a book. The acceptance of some individual poems by a few magazines gave him the courage to move ahead. With money from the sale of the farm and his annuity, he decided to dedicate time to becoming a poet.

Frost thought he would benefit from a change of location and wanted to go to either Canada or England. Elinor favored England because she wanted to live under a thatched roof. They decided to rest their decision on the flip of a coin. "The coin chose England," Frost said. With its literary reputation and resources, Frost believed that England could provide the ideal

The SS Parisian, *the steamship on which the Frost family traveled to England in 1912.* (Library of Congress)

environment for him to develop as a poet. He resigned his job at the college, and by August 12, 1912, the family was ready to depart. Temporarily leaving behind his wife and four children, who ranged in age from seven to thirteen, Frost went to Boston to prepare for them to make the trip to England. The family took only minimal personal belongings and joined Frost in Boston a week later. As they sailed away on August 24 aboard the SS *Parisian*, few Americans knew or cared that Robert Frost had left the country.

After arriving in London in September, the family looked for affordable housing. They finally settled in a small cottage in Beaconsfield, twenty miles north of London. The rent was $20 per month. Another $125 bought basic second-hand furniture for the Bungalow, the name they gave their home. At first the neighbors were suspicious of the Americans who had moved to their village. Having no friends, the family spent most of its time together, and life in the Bungalow resembled life on the Derry farm. Daughter Lesley later recalled, "My mother never worked alone in the kitchen. We all congregated around the stove or the ironing board or the sewing basket and *talked.*"

Frost visited the local schools to find the best places for his children's education, but large class sizes of forty or more students per room disappointed him. Since he could not afford private school for all four children, he and Elinor decided that the two of them would educate Marjorie and Carol at home. They sent the two older girls, Lesley and Irma, to a private school called St. Anne's.

During this period, Frost concentrated on pulling together his first collection of poetry. He was very aware of the passing years: "I wasn't going to pass forty without having it out with myself on this score [of becoming a published poet]." The idea for his first volume, *A Boy's Will,* came one night after everyone had gone to bed.

Frost sat on the floor in front of the fireplace. Around him he spread out over one hundred poems, some of them dating back to his high school days. As if dealing a deck of cards, he stacked them in various combinations and discarded those that no longer interested him. With the remaining poems, he started looking for a unifying theme. He settled on a three-part arrangement that showed a young man's long search for artistic direction. A spiral of moods moving from discouragement and withdrawal to hope and affirmation detailed the quest. As he sat there with the poems scattered around him, Frost recalled the poem "My Lost Youth" by the American poet Henry Wadsworth Longfellow. It seemed to illustrate the inconsistencies in Frost's own life up to this point:

A boy's will is the wind's will
And the thoughts of youth are long, long thoughts.

Frost decided to use seasonal elements—a move from autumn to autumn—to add another dimension to the changing moods of the collection. In the initial version, he wrote commentaries to lead the reader through the changes that had occurred in his life and in his writing. In a letter to a friend, Frost said that *A Boy's Will* "comes pretty near being the story of five years of my life." Under this guiding theme, Frost put together thirty-two poems. They contained references to the natural elements that became a hallmark of his poetry: stars, clouds, flowers, leaves, brooks, and birds. Frost himself described the book as "a series of lyrics standing in some such loose relation to each other as a ring of children who have just stopped dancing and let go hands." He was still developing his ideas about everyday language and poetry, so the poems contain old-fashioned terms like "they wist" (they know) and "that frighted thee so oft."

With the poems selected, and with Elinor's encouragement, Frost headed to London to look for a publisher.

The only person that he knew in London was a retired policeman who had helped the Frosts in their search for living quarters. The man, who worked at the office of *T.P.'s Weekly,* offered Frost the name of a vanity publisher—a company that takes payment from writers to publish their books. When Frost declined that type of publication, the man mentioned the firm of David Nutt, a small but noted publisher of many popular British poets of that time.

Mrs. M. L. Nutt headed the firm that she had inherited upon her husband's death. When Frost approached her, she said simply that she would read the manuscript. Several days later she notified him that her firm wanted to publish *A Boy's Will.* In recalling that news, Frost's daughter Lesley said, "We [the children] were pleased because our elders seemed pleased. We couldn't comprehend . . . what resolve, what hope, what patience in waiting, had gone into that first book: what a climax, what a beginning, was signified by such a recognition coming at last."

In the excitement of getting his first book published, Frost did not make careful decisions about the future financial significance of the terms Mrs. Nutt offered. First, in signing the contract for *A Boy's Will,* Frost agreed to help pay the costs of publishing. Of more impact was her desire for the option to publish his next four books, poetry or prose. Frost agreed and signed the contract on December 16. She said that the book would be on store shelves by February of 1913.

four

England's Literary World

The acceptance of his first book spurred Frost's imagination. He began a sustained period of writing and in just a few months, he wrote a dozen or more lengthy poems. Frost also began to venture out and make connections with London's literary world. In January, he attended the Poetry Bookshop opening, hosted by its owner Harold Monro. Among the three hundred people attending the opening was Frank Flint, a poet who had received good reviews for his first book three years earlier. Frost bought a copy of Flint's book and asked him to sign it. While Flint was doing so, Frost told him about his own forthcoming publication. Flint offered to review the book but more importantly offered to arrange a meeting between Frost and Ezra Pound, another American poet living in London.

American expatriate poet and critic, Ezra Pound. (Library of Congress)

Ezra Pound had studied romance languages in the United States before going to England in 1908 to study with the great Irish poet William Butler Yeats. Pound, who had self-published several volumes before leaving the United States, found a rush of creativity during the next three years in England, publishing six collections. He possessed wide-ranging contacts in the arts and served as an editor, advocate, and sponsor of other writers.

Pound was also the English representative for a new American monthly magazine called *Poetry,* published in Chicago by Harriet Monroe. Frost knew that Pound reviewed books, and he had heard that the only way to get a book of poetry reviewed was through personal contacts. Frost believed that if Pound so chose, he could not only write a review of Frost's book but also introduce Frost to leading literary figures in London. However, shortly after reaching out to Pound, Frost was not quite sure what to think when he received a card that read: "At home—sometimes." A week before *A Boy's Will* was due in the stores, Frost made a visit.

Pound answered the door wearing a dressing gown. He demanded to know why Frost had waited so long to come by and where his copy of the book was. Frost had not yet received any copies, so Pound suggested that just as soon as he dressed, they walk to the publisher's office. The firm offered them one copy of the book, which Pound took in his own hands. Frost never even got to touch that first copy.

Through his association with Pound, Frost met some of the best-known writers in England, including Yeats, whom Frost had admired for years. After reading *A Boy's Will*, Yeats said that it was "the best poetry written in America for a long time."

At the Poetry Bookshop, where London's writers gathered, Frost became acquainted with many of the so-called Georgian poets. Frost aligned himself both personally and professionally with this group, though his poetry was often darker than the rustic sentimentality of the British Georgian poets.

The Georgian poets took their name from England's George V, who was crowned in 1911. Usually inspired by nature, they wrote light, sentimental lyrics about friendship and love, in contrast to the nineteenth-century Victorian poets, who often wrote about the social problems of the day. Critics hailed Georgian poetry as a rebellion in English literature, challenging the formal diction, wordiness, and artificial sentiment of earlier writers.

Georgians rejected the drab repetition of urban life and tried to find in the countryside the color, romance, and simplicity that industrialization had banished from the average Briton's existence. Their verse concentrated on idealized rural themes contrasted with the poverty, ugliness, and unrest of urban decay.

Among the best-known Georgian poets were Rupert Brooke, Robert Graves, Lascelles Abercrombie, Walter de la Mare, D. H. Lawrence, and Siegfried Sassoon. Their work appeared in a series of five anthologies called *Georgian Poetry*, edited by Edward Marsh and published by Harold Monro. Although considered revolutionary, within ten years the Georgians were supplanted by more modern poets, such as T. S. Eliot. His monumental work, *The Waste Land,* depicted society as isolated and decadent. Appearing about the same time as the last Georgian anthology, the poem was hailed as the onset of modernism. Modernism rejected the emphasis on beauty and man's response to it in order to present what the new group of poets believed was a truer picture of how people felt and thought.

This period also saw the rise of another poetry movement, its adherents known as imagists. Frost never iden-

The original 1913 cover of Frost's first collection of poems, A Boy's Will, *published by David Nutt.* (Library of Congress)

tified himself with these poets. Ezra Pound, an early leader of this group, preached modernization, especially through experimentation with free verse forms. When Pound pressured Frost to write in free verse, or *vers libre*, Frost responded, "I had as soon write free verse as play tennis with the net down." Frost felt that free verse, with its lack of rhyme and varied line lengths, ignored too many of the conventional poetical forms. He believed that following the established rules was part of the fun in any game. Despite these disagreements, Frost could not have been in a better place than England to be able to interact with the literary leaders of the time.

Two weeks after the publication of *A Boy's Will*, not a single review had appeared. Frost knew the book would sell only if it received positive reviews. The apparent lack of interest shook his self-confidence. When the first review finally appeared on the back page of *Athenaeum*, a literary weekly, it was not encouraging. The next review, which appeared in the *Times Literary Supplement*, was lukewarm at best: "There is an agreeable individuality about these pieces; the writer is not afraid to voice the simplest of his thoughts and fancies, and these, springing from a capacity for complete absorption in the influences of nature and the open air, are often naively engaging. Sometimes too, in a vein of reflection, he makes one stop and think, though the thought may be feebly or obscurely expressed." As other brief reviews appeared, Pound's eventually among them, Frost felt disappointed that most of the reviewers saw his poems as simple.

Pound's and Frost's association lasted only a few months. Frost did not like Pound's disagreeable attitude but hesitated to sever their relationship too soon. Pound had Frost's original manuscript of the poem "The Death of the Hired Man" and had promised to send it to *Poetry*.

Instead he sent it to *The Smart Set* in New York, not the kind of magazine in which Frost wanted his poem published. Fortunately for Frost, the magazine rejected the poem.

With the early mixed reviews pushing him again toward depression, Frost took his family on a brief trip to Scotland. The sight of stone walls there reminded him of his Derry farm and deepened his homesickness. He appreciated New England more now that he was abroad.

When the family returned to England, Frost learned that three more reviews of *A Boy's Will*, all positive, had been published while he was in Scotland. An unnamed reviewer wrote in the *Academy*: "One feels that this man has *seen* and *felt*; seen with a . . . creative vision; felt personally and intensely; and he simply writes down, without confusion . . . the results thereof. . . . No one who cares for poetry should miss this little book."

Now, Mrs. Nutt decided to publish a second volume of Frost's poetry. The reviews and the promise of a second book not only gave Frost more confidence but also lifted his fog of homesickness. Suddenly, he began to think about a life in America in which he could support his family with his poetry. He wrote to his friend Sidney Cox, "My dream would be to get the thing started in London and then do the rest of it from a farm in New England where I could live cheap and get Yankier and Yankier."

Before that vision could become reality, Frost knew that he had to establish a strong reputation in London.

British critic Edward Thomas was important to Frost both as a friend and as an intelligent reader who understood the originality of Frost's work.

He continued to mingle with other poets and found a friend in the critic Edward Thomas. Frost recognized the poetic qualities in Thomas's prose and encouraged him to start writing poetry.

Two of the Georgians, Wilfred Gibson and Lascelles Abercrombie, invited Frost and his family to move to Gloucestershire. Since Frost had wanted to leave Beaconsfield for some time and enjoy the English countryside, he accepted the invitation. After finding another family willing to take over the lease at Beaconsfield, Frost found a cottage, known as Little Iddens, surrounded by fruit orchards, hayfields, and meadows. The family arrived at Little Iddens in April 1914 and immediately fell in love with the fields of daffodils, flocks of sheep, and pear trees that dropped white snowflake leaves.

Frost's only concern about moving was that he would be away from London when the reviews of his second book appeared. All the poems were set in the New England landscape, and Frost had compared the physical isolation of that region to the mental isolation suffered by many of its inhabitants. The volume, titled *North of Boston,* contained dramatic narratives and monologues begun in America and polished in England. It also featured several lyric poems composed in Beaconsfield—"Birches," "Mending Wall," and "After Apple-Picking"—written in response to Frost's homesickness for the New England he had left behind.

Little Iddens, the house where the Frost family stayed from April of 1914 through February of 1915.

Thematically, the poems covered a wide range: the difficulties and possibilities of human communication, death, the isolation of the individual, and the oppression of the past. The poems' speakers always seemed on the verge of learning something important about themselves. The teacher was nature, and the epiphany was almost within reach but elusive. Because nothing in nature ever stood still, knowledge was never complete. In "The Wood-Pile," the speaker walks aimlessly through a cold, stark winter landscape. At one point he pauses, debating whether to turn back toward old, familiar ground or to go farther:

> Out walking in the frozen swamp one gray day,
> I paused and said, "I will turn back from here.
> No, I will go on farther—and we shall see."

Deciding to see what lies ahead, the speaker moves ahead deep in thought. He comes upon a deserted woodpile and stops to consider what happened to the man who used an ax to cut and split the now-decaying wood. Did the man die? Or did he just leave his task and turn to new challenges? Trying to solve the riddle, the traveler thinks about the limitations of his own knowledge and recognizes the human capacity for wasteful extravagance—to mark a barren landscape with a structure like the woodpile and then abandon it. Then he observes that nature has taken the human waste and ordered it into another form so that the woodpile, with its rotting wood, serves an unintended purpose:

To warm the frozen swamp as best it could
With the slow smokeless burning of decay.

The speaker tries to infer some intention or design from what he observes, but all he can do is acknowledge that nature is independent of human need or perception. Nature poses the questions in his mind but has no answers for him.

With the publication of his second book, Frost hoped also to clarify the "sound of sense" theory with which he had struggled since the criticism in his younger days that his poetry sounded too much like conversation. Frost believed that what the reader often missed in literature was the sentence sounds beneath the words. He wanted to give equal value to the eye that saw and to the ear that heard. Frost felt that the way words sound is more important than the actual words themselves because even though the reader / listener cannot always understand the words, the tones of voice tell whether the person speaking in the poem is angry, hurt, joyful, pleading, demanding, or doubtful. He said, "A sentence *must* convey a meaning by tone of voice and it must be the particular meaning the writer intended. The reader must have no choice in the matter."

One of Frost's favorite verse forms was blank verse, a pattern of five alternating unaccented and accented syllables per unrhymed line. To achieve the sound of speech, Frost frequently broke the meter and made the

Opposite: *Frost in England in 1913.* (Courtesy of Dartmouth College Library.)

lines uneven. Frost used these techniques in such poems as "The Death of the Hired Man" to give full range to the emotional content:

"Home," he mocked gently.
                              "Yes, what else but home?
It all depends on what you mean by home.
. . . .
"Home is the place where, when you have to go there,
They have to take you in."
                              "I should have called it
Something you somehow haven't to deserve."

In the spring, Frost's new friend Edward Thomas and Thomas's son Mervyn came for a week's visit in Gloucestershire. Although the family enjoyed long walks during the children's vacation from school, tension filled the air. *North of Boston* had been in the stores for two weeks, and there were no reviews. Then another guest arrived and brought with him several reviews. A critic for the *Times Literary Supplement* wrote: "Poetry burns up out of it—as when a faint wind breathes upon smouldering embers." For the first time critics mentioned Frost's sound of sense: "Poetry, in this book, seems determined . . . to invigorate itself by utilizing the traits and necessities of common life, the habits of common speech, the minds and hearts of common folk."

Pleased with the success of his second book, Frost hoped the publication of a third would cement his reputation in England and allow him to return to America as an established literary figure. In August 1914, England responded to Germany's invasion of Belgium by declaring war. Most Britons believed the conflict would be settled by Christmas, so, after some debate, Frost decided his family would be safe enough in England.

Frost's friendship with Edward Thomas proved fruitful as Thomas published admiring reviews of *North of Boston* in three different magazines, solidifying Frost's reputation. Then, in September 1914, the New York publishing firm of Henry Holt contacted Mrs. Nutt about obtaining the American rights to *North of Boston* as well as to any of Frost's future works. Mrs. Nutt agreed to send Holt the unbound pages of the manuscript with permission to make 150 copies. Despite the small number, Frost was overjoyed that an American publisher had shown an interest in his poetry. He told Elinor, "Now we can go home, the book has gone home."

The news could not have come at a better time. Rumors abounded that Germany planned a blockade of British ports. If the Frosts did not leave soon, they might not be able to do so. Unfortunately, Robert could not afford passage for a family of six. He thought about asking for an advance on his annuity. If he did that, the family would have no money to live on the next year in the United States. Determined that his career as a poet must have priority, Frost borrowed travel money from three English friends.

He arranged for the family to sail from Liverpool, England, on February 13, 1915, aboard the American liner *St. Paul.* The Frosts took Edward Thomas's fifteen-year-old son Mervyn with them. His father feared that Germany was going to invade Britain, and he wanted his son in a safe place.

When they left the harbor, the threat of German sabotage filled their minds as a convoy of British destroyers surrounded their ship. Less than two months later, German torpedoes would blow up the British ship *Lusitania,* following the same course, killing 1,195 people.

As a writer he could live anywhere, but Frost knew that he wanted to return to New England, the place that had supplied the inspiration for so much of his poetry. Frost worried about whether he could provide for his family with the income from royalties. His self-confidence wavered as he wondered how many more books he could write. He probably had enough poems for one more volume, but what if his creative powers dried up? He recalled Ezra Pound's review of *North of Boston* in which he criticized American editors for not having recognized Frost's talent first and openly ridiculed some of the most distinguished poets in the U.S. Frost worried that editors would think Pound's ideas were Frost's opinions as well and that they would boycott Frost's books. His thoughts and insecurities churned like the seas that carried him home.

five

Unknown at Home

In 1915, after two and a half years abroad, the Frosts finally returned to American soil. The family stayed at a New York hotel while they made plans for the future. Frost stopped at a newsstand in the city, where he idly leafed through a copy of the *The New Republic,* a journal whose circulation had grown to over 14,000 in its first year of publication. To his surprise, Frost discovered a lengthy review of *North of Boston* by the American poet Amy Lowell. The wealthy, prominent socialite and poet was well entrenched in Boston as a literary leader, belonging to the same family line as the noted poet James Russell Lowell. Her brother was president of Harvard University. She called the book "the most American volume of poetry which has appeared for some time."

Poet and critic Amy Lowell.
(Library of Congress)

Frost could not spend much time reveling in her acclaim. He needed to get his family settled. He contacted John Lynch, who had a farm in the White Mountains between Bethlehem and Franconia, New Hampshire. The Frosts had spent several summer vacations with the Lynches, and Mr. Lynch assured Frost that his family was welcome to rent rooms again. However, Edward Thomas's son Mervyn had run into some immigration problems at Ellis Island. Either a parent or a sponsor with proven financial ability to support another person had to meet any alien under age sixteen at the immigration office. Initially, since Frost could not prove that he had a job, the officials would not accept him as Mervyn's sponsor. Frost could not leave the boy alone until the situation was resolved, so only Elinor and the four children went on to the Lynches' farm.

While he waited for a solution to Mervyn's problem, Frost visited the offices of his American publisher, Henry Holt and Company. From them he learned that his poem "The Death of the Hired Man" had been sold to *The New Republic* for forty dollars. He also met Florence Taber Holt, who first discovered *North of Boston* and encouraged her husband to print it in America.

When Mervyn's immigration problems were finally settled, Frost put him on a train to his relatives. Before heading to New Hampshire, Frost decided to make a surprise visit to see his sister Jeanie, a teacher. Her last letter had come from Wildwood, New Jersey, so Frost took a train there only to learn that she had been fired and was now teaching in South Fork, Pennsylvania, three hundred miles to the west. Frost was not too surprised; he had learned from her infrequent letters that she usually held a teaching job for only a year before moving on. Her nervous, depressed state of mind made it difficult for her to deal with unruly students.

When they finally caught up, Jeanie seemed glad to see her brother. Frost encouraged his sister to go back to college, and despite his own limited means, he offered financial assistance for her to do so if she needed it.

From Pennsylvania, Frost traveled to Massachusetts, where he collected a $200 advance on the annuity left to him by his grandfather and visited the offices of *The Atlantic Monthly,* a popular literary and cultural magazine dedicated to the expression of New England thought. Frost had long desired publication in this magazine, but the editors had never shown any interest in his work. This time the editor, Ellery Sedgwick, greeted Frost cordially and invited him to dinner that evening to meet some of Sedgwick's friends. When members of the Boston Author's Club learned that Frost was in town, they asked Sedgwick for an introduction, since they planned to discuss Frost's work at their next meeting. In Boston, Frost also met and had dinner with poet-critic Amy Lowell, who had written such a positive review of *North of Boston*. Although she was patronizing in her manner, Frost expressed his gratitude and made a favorable impression before he left.

When Frost finally joined his family in New Hampshire, he glowed with the success of his Boston visits. But he still had to solve the problem of finding a place to live and getting the children enrolled in school. Frost decided on a small farm in Franconia, New Hampshire, near Sugar Hill. Like other places the family had lived, the property had all kinds of trees, pastures, and a barn. The house itself, however, lacked indoor plumbing and electricity. A wood stove in the kitchen heated the cottage while an uphill spring provided water. Despite these primitive conditions, the family liked the farm, and Frost closed the deal with a handshake.

The Boston literary community continued to reach out to Frost, and he received several invitations to read his poetry, including one from the Boston Author's Club. He also met the poet-critic Louis Untermeyer, a noted book reviewer and a contributing editor to *The Masses*,

Frost writes at his desk on the farm in Franconia, New Hampshire, 1915.
(Courtesy of Dartmouth College Library.)

a socialist magazine published in Greenwich Village, New York. The two were brought together by their mutual friend, Lascelles Abercrombie. Untermeyer later wrote a review for the *Chicago Evening Post* in which he praised *North of Boston*. This began an association that continued over the lifetimes of the two men, as Untermeyer encouraged and supported Frost's writing. In hundreds of letters that the two wrote to each other for almost half a century, Frost shared his personal life and his poetic thoughts. Untermeyer wrote and edited over one hundred books, including anthologies of American and British literature.

The days gradually took on a pattern for Frost—farming, family time, writing, and "barding around," as he called his lecturing and poetry reading. He had a brief schedule of appearances in the Boston area, and after that he had occasional invitations to lecture at various universities, including Dartmouth. These tours gave him much-needed extra income.

Elinor became pregnant a seventh time and fell quite ill in the fall of 1915. Since her doctor had warned her not to have more children because of her weak heart, her miscarriage in November was a relief to her husband. That fall and spring, Frost's invitations to speak increased, and he lectured widely. Then Harvard, the school from which he had walked away as a young man, asked him to read a poem at their commencement exercises.

This invitation filled him with new energy, and he began work on his third book, *Mountain Interval,* a term that referred to the valleys between hills. He had already written most of the poems; he just needed to decide their order in the book. In November 1916, Holt published the book. Almost all of the thirty-two poems derived their subject matter from the farms where the Frost family had lived. *Mountain Interval* combined elements of both of Frost's previous volumes. Three-fourths of the poems were lyrics like those found in *A Boy's Will* while the others resembled the dramatic narratives of *North of Boston. Mountain Interval* introduced a new element—the poet's talking to his readers in a conversational, fanciful tone as he explained his attitudes toward life.

Major Types of Poetry

The major types of poetry are lyric, narrative, and dramatic. Lyric poems express thoughts or emotions in a song-like form. The earliest lyric poetry developed in ancient Greece, where music played on a harp-like instrument called a lyre accompanied the poem.

Most of today's lyric poems are short poems that make an impact in a brief space by stressing a moment of feeling.

Sonnets and odes are types of lyric poems. The sonnet is a fourteen-line poem usually written in iambic pentameter and following one of several strict rhyme schemes. The ode is a long poem, usually serious, with formal, dignified language, elaborate figures of speech, and a formal stanza structure. Imagery in a skillfully written lyric poem can evoke the reader's remembrance of a similar experience.

Narrative verse tells a story by giving an account of an event or a series of real or imagined events. Narrative poetry is the oldest type of poetry, having its origin in the oral traditions of ancient peoples. The earliest narrative poems were intended to be spoken aloud. Poetic techniques, such as rhyme and meter, enabled poets to memorize large numbers of poems.

Dramatic poems reveal the thoughts and/or spoken comments of one or more characters. The poems employ such elements of drama as dialogue, conflict, and characterization. Dramatic poems do not require a set stanza form, and the poet may choose any metrical or rhyme pattern. A story told by a single character is a dramatic monologue. The character, by speaking aloud, allows other characters and/or the reader to listen to his innermost thoughts.

Although each of these types of poems has its own features, a poem may contain characteristics of more than one type.

The opening poem of *Mountain Interval,* "The Road Not Taken," showcased Frost's developing style. Although Frost said that he wrote the poem as a satirical response to his friend Edward Thomas's inability to make a decision, readers interpreted it in a more metaphysical sense—the poet's describing an incident in the physical world which turned into thoughts that transcended to the world of emotion and of the spirit.

> I shall be telling this with a sigh
> Somewhere ages and ages hence:
> Two roads diverged in a wood, and I—
> I took the one less traveled by,
> And that has made all the difference.

In reviewing *Mountain Interval,* Frost's friend Sidney Cox called sincerity the fundamental quality of the book—"sincerity in perception, sincerity in thought, sincerity in feeling and sincerity in expression." However, the book was not received with great enthusiasm. Louis Untermeyer, in trying to explain why the book never achieved the popularity of the first two, said it lacked unity, even though it contained some of the poet's finest works. Although Frost once referred to the book as just a bunch of poems slapped together, the poems continued to develop the same themes of isolation, loneliness, death, and fear.

Only a month after the publication of *Mountain Interval,* President Alexander Meiklejohn of Amherst College extended an invitation to Frost to take a position on the school's faculty in spring 1917. For a salary of $2,000, Frost would have to teach only two classes. He could continue his readings and lectures at other universities. Frost was torn. Before Frost left England, he had written to Sidney Cox, "I should awfully like a quiet job in a small college where I should be allowed to teach something a little new on the technique of writing and where I should have some honor for what I suppose myself to have done in poetry." Frost knew that the demands of teaching interfered with his writing, but *Mountain Interval* was not selling well. Frost accepted the job. That same spring, Frost received word that his good friend Edward Thomas, at the age of thirty-nine, had died in a World War I battle from a German shell's direct hit. Thomas had joined the Royal Garrison Artillery in July 1915 because he felt responsibility, as a British subject, to fight the Germans. As he moved from camp to camp, he and Frost kept in touch, and Frost had encouraged him to continue writing.

Frost took pride in Thomas's development as a poet and convinced Alfred Harcourt to publish some of his friend's poems in the United States. Because of his reputation as a critic, Thomas wrote his poetry under the pseudonym Edward Eastaway. After Thomas's death, Frost asked Helen Thomas to release the poems under her husband's real name. She declined because that was not what Thomas wanted. In a letter to another friend, Frost wrote, "Edward Thomas was the only brother I ever had. . . . I hadn't a plan for the future that didn't include him."

Founded in 1821, Amherst College is located in Amherst, Massachusetts, a small, picturesque town in the western part of the state. (Library of Congress)

In the fall of 1917, the Frost family moved to Amherst. They settled in a house within walking distance of the college and enrolled the children in school. The year was not a productive one for Frost as a poet. However, his name appeared in such respected publications as *The Atlantic Monthly* and Amy Lowell's new book, *Tendencies in Modern American Poetry.*

Before the end of Frost's first term at Amherst, the United States had entered World War I, and by September 1918, the War Department had taken over the college to create a Students' Army Training Corps that dictated classroom curriculum. Many of Frost's students dropped out to join the service. Frost frequently argued about war with those remaining. He believed in the rightness and

The Frost home on Sunset Avenue in Amherst, Massachusetts. (Courtesy of Dartmouth College Library.)

inevitability of war as a means of final resolution of differences between nations. Anyone who favored pacifism received Frost's outspoken disgust.

Several times Frost approached Amherst's president about returning to his farm, and each time Meiklejohn offered a new lure to keep him—first, a full professorship, and then an honorary degree at commencement in 1918. In the fall of that year, a terrible flu epidemic killed nearly 700,000 people within the United States, 20 million worldwide. Frost became seriously sick and missed ten weeks of teaching. He was too ill to celebrate the end of World War I on November 11. Elinor struggled to care for her sick husband and their four children.

Frost was unhappy not to be writing much poetry while at Amherst and made matters more difficult for himself by trying to have Stark Young, the English department chair, fired because he was gay. Faculty and students supported Young, and the president refused to get rid of him. In protest, Frost announced that he would resign after graduation. In July, he wrote to Sidney Cox, "I've kicked myself out of Amherst and settled down to revising old poems when I'm not making new ones. . . . If you ever see any talk of me in print you may notice that it is my frostiness that is more and more played up."

Now Frost had to figure out how he was going to provide for his family. Although he received numerous invitations to lecture, he usually netted only about $100 for each performance. He had published a mere half-dozen poems in the past three years. Back in Franconia, he decided that the climate did not lend itself to farming. He began to look for another farm. He received an offer of $2,500 for half the Franconian farm, with the option of the buyer's purchasing the other half at some future time if Frost wanted to sell. That arrangement allowed Frost to buy another farm he had discovered in South Shaftsbury, Vermont. Getting back to farm life had a positive effect on Frost's creativity, and during the summer and fall of 1920, he wrote six important poems, among them "Fire and Ice." He completed several other poems that he had begun earlier, such as "Nothing Gold Can Stay," and with the combination of new and old he had almost enough for another collection.

In the midst of this resurgence of writing, Frost received word that his sister Jeanie had been taken into police custody in Portland, Maine. After Frost's offer to help her financially, Jeanie had returned to college and completed her studies in two and a half years. But the war disturbed her already troubled mental state. For years, in various states of paranoia, she had believed underworld figures wanted to kidnap her for the white-slave trade.

Her problem in Portland began at a drugstore's pay telephone. Jeanie tried to call the family lawyer, Wilbur Rowell, to get an advance on her annuity. When she could not reach him, she became hysterical. The pharmacist called the police, and Jeanie strongly resisted them because she believed that they were kidnapping her. After they subdued her, the police took Jeanie to jail, placed her in a cell, and called a doctor. The physician examined her and gave her some medicine to calm her down. He said that she should be put in an insane asylum.

Not having a contact number for her brother, the police notified Wilbur Rowell. The lawyer wrote a letter to Frost, informing him of the situation. Frost did not know what to do. Placing his sister in a mental institution was a drastic step, but he knew that he and Elinor could not care for her. Frost himself experienced frequent fits of extreme anxiety, and Jeanie's mental state deeply concerned him. He wrote the attorney, "My hope is that what has been pronounced insanity may turn out no more than the strange mixture of hysteria and eccentricity she has shown us so much of."

The two had been highly competitive until they entered high school. There, Jeanie had withdrawn into her own make-believe world, often descending into periods of depression. After their mother died, Jeanie's condition worsened. She made some terrible scenes in front of Frost's young children. Since those episodes, brother and sister had not seen much of each other.

Although Frost worried about his sister, he had not thought she was insane. He took a train to Portland, but when he arrived, Jeanie did not recognize him. Doctors convinced Frost that his sister belonged in the state mental hospital. He signed the commitment papers.

At first, Frost made several trips to visit Jeanie. All of their encounters were painful. Frost could tell that both her physical condition and her state of mind were growing worse. They corresponded some, and Frost sent Jeanie the little gifts that she requested.

In the early 1920s, overcrowded wards and chronic understaffing characterized mental institutions, and mental illness was often considered a personal failing rather than an illness. Placement in an institution was primarily for custodial care. Electroshock therapy, where doctors administer electric current into a patient, and lobotomy, where nerve endings in the brain are severed, were among procedures used to stabilize mental behavior. Only toward the very end of Jeanie's lifetime did psychiatry become a field that sought medical solutions for mental diseases. Jeanie Frost stayed in the mental institution for the rest of her life and died there in 1929.

After giving a brief three-session course in reading and writing at Bryn Mawr College in November, Frost visited Holt, his publisher, in New York. Alfred Harcourt and Donald Brace, heads of the trade and production departments at Holt, had just resigned to start their own publishing company. They actively pursued many of Holt's current authors, including Frost.

Frost attempted to sever his contract with Holt in order to go with Harcourt and Brace. Holt reminded Frost of how the company had worked hard to get the American rights to his first two books and that they also had *Mountain Interval* under copyright. If Frost left Holt, he could never include the poems from those three volumes in any book of collected works. To soften his refusal to release Frost, Holt offered Frost a position as consulting editor at a salary of $100 per month. The job was intended to supply additional income for Frost and required little or no work.

Frost agreed and continued to accept all invitations to speak. As he traveled widely across the United States, he also began to look for another connection to a college or university. He wanted a less restrictive appointment. That summer he taught at the newly opened School of English at Bread Loaf Mountain, outside Middlebury, Vermont. About the same time, he received an invitation from the University of Michigan at Ann Arbor to spend a year as a poet-in-residence at a salary of $5,000. Frost knew that acceptance meant another move for his family. But they needed the money, and Frost needed the stimulation of being around literary people.

The Frosts found a large, furnished Victorian house in Ann Arbor. Nineteen-year-old Marjorie, who was a junior in high school, did not come with them, staying behind with her best friend Lillian LaBatt in order to continue at North Bennington High School. Twenty-two-year-old Carol remained on the farm at South Shaftsbury for a while to tend the apple crop. Lesley, at age twenty-five, had been working as a book dealer in New York but decided to join the family and audit a few courses at the university. Twenty-one-year-old Irma also planned to audit some courses in art history but wanted to focus mainly on her painting and sculpture, working in a large studio on the top floor of their house.

After arriving in Michigan in the fall of 1921, the university allowed Frost to design his position. One of his main goals was to bring other writers of importance to the university campus. Carl Sandburg, Amy Lowell, Vachel Lindsay, Padraic Colum, and Louis Untermeyer all visited the campus during his tenure there. Frost himself spent little time on the campus as he continued a heavy schedule of readings and lectures. At the same time, he was working with a new editor at Holt on a fourth volume of poetry called *New Hampshire.*

This collection, his first in seven years, revealed Frost as master of the metaphor. Frost did not set out to compare one thing in terms of another, for example, dark

NEW HAMPSHIRE
A POEM WITH NOTES
AND GRACE NOTES BY
ROBERT FROST
WITH WOODCUTS
BY J. J. LANKES
PUBLISHED BY
HENRY HOLT
& COMPANY : NEW
YORK : MCMXXIII

woods to death. Rather, he let his mind slowly absorb the significant details of an experience and then waited for that experience to reveal a truth that suggested something deeper than the surface words. Frost explained, "A poem is an idea dawning. If you have it before you write it, it will be like translating it into poetry; but if you feel it as it is making in your mind, then it is a poem. If it hasn't that freshness of dawn on it, it isn't a good poem."

Frost believed that metaphors grow out of things "cutting across one another and making a connection in the mind." Therefore, he looked for images and experiences common to human beings but uncommon in poetry. Out of these he developed metaphors about New England people's strengths and weaknesses, highlighting the peculiar character of these people in their particular environment—stone walls, frozen woods, cellar holes.

In the tradition of other metaphysical poets, Frost took the most insignificant natural fact and used it as a vehicle to move to universal thoughts and emotions. In most of his poems Frost seemed to wait on the moment when the physical fact and the mystery that surrounded it seemed to cross. One of the best examples of Frost's use of metaphor is found in the closing lines of "Stopping by Woods on a Snowy Evening," a poem in the *New Hampshire* collection:

> The woods are lovely, dark, and deep,
> But I have promises to keep,
> And miles to go before I sleep,
> And miles to go before I sleep.

On the surface the speaker stopped to look at the beauty of the dark woods but realized that he could not linger because of commitments he had. By repeating the third line, Frost made a metaphysical extension to the promises of the spirit, not those of the ordinary world implied in the third line. The speaker is a lonely man reacting to the spiritual pull of the symbols of death around him. Although the dark woods entice him to linger there, the speaker returns to the real world, mindful of this life's obligations.

In *New Hampshire,* Frost broadened his vision to express some of his philosophical beliefs. For example,

Stopping by Woods on a Snowy Evening
Whose woods these are I think I know.
His house is in the village though.
He will not see me stopping here
To watch his woods fill up with snow.

My little horse must think it queer
To stop without a farmhouse near
Between the woods and frozen lake
The darkest evening of the year.

He gives his harness bells a shake
To ask if there is some mistake.
The only other sound's the sweep
Of easy wind and downy flake

The woods are lovely, dark and deep.
But I have promises to keep,
And miles to go before I sleep —
And miles to go before I sleep.

Robert Frost

This copy of Frost's famous poem "Stopping By Woods on a Snowy Evening" was written in Frost's own hand. (Library of Congress) in "Nothing Gold Can Stay," he presented one of his favorite themes: the inevitability of change. To illustrate, he used the green of nature, the dawn's beauty, and the initial perfection in the Garden of Eden. Knowing that all of these settings are transitory, Frost believed that man should enjoy each moment before it passes and not waste time lamenting that which cannot be changed. The human condition must accept that life's gains and losses always bring a mingling of joy and sorrow:

Metaphysical Poetry

The term metaphysical, when applied to poetry, goes back to the seventeenth century, when it was originally a derogatory term leveled against writers whose complicated poems could be understood by only a few readers. Later, Dr. Samuel Johnson used the expression to describe a number of poets who used similar techniques, including the building of an extended comparison between two seemingly unrelated things or events; a witty, clever tone; use of contradictions; informal language; a tendency to dramatize situations; rejection of overly romantic or idyllic theories; and a love of philosophic topics.

Metaphysical poetry often explores such topics as man's significance and his role in nature. Early metaphysical poets, like John Donne, rebelled against conventional imagery. The metaphysical poets used complex poems to explore their sense of life's complications and contradictions. Their tool for this was the metaphysical conceit, a clever and fanciful metaphor generally expressed through an elaborate and extended comparison, such as comparing a beautiful woman to a garden or the sun.

Nature's first green is gold,
Her hardest hue to hold.
Her early leaf's a flower;
But only so an hour.
Then leaf subsides to leaf.
So Eden sank to grief,
So dawn goes down to day.
Nothing gold can stay.

Another unique feature of *New Hampshire* was that it was the first of Frost's books to contain illustrations, woodcuts by J. J. Lankes. Critics and the public alike praised this fourth volume of Frost's verse, for which Frost received the 1923 Pulitzer Prize for poetry, an award for the best book of poems published in the United States that year. That award paved the way for his first honorary doctorate in letters, from Yale University.

With these recognitions, Frost firmly established himself among the country's literary elite. But this wealth of public success did not translate to his family.

six

"The Door in the Dark"

In 1923, Frost had entered into a two-year commitment to teach again at Amherst, a campus that continued to draw him back despite his previous issues with the college. Frost had left Amherst because he disliked the liberal atmosphere fostered by President Meiklejohn, in which a diverse array of views was not only tolerated but also encouraged. In Frost's absence, a majority of the faculty had protested Meiklejohn's discouragement of religion on campus and his mismanagement of his personal and college funds. As part of the dissenting faculty, Stark Young, with whom Frost had clashed, resigned. The board dismissed Meiklejohn. With both Meiklejohn and Young gone, Frost was happy to return to the campus to help shape its liberal arts curriculum.

One of Frost's colleagues described him as "a born

teacher with a knack of charging dry subjects with intellectual excitement and a large patience for struggling learners." Frost taught only one course. He told his students to read deeply for ideas and to write about their reading only if they had something to say. That same year, Henry Holt and Company published *Selected Poems*, and Frost's son Carol married Lillian LaBatt, his sister Marjorie's best friend, who happened to be partially deaf. Since the Frosts lived near Amherst, they gave the young couple the South Shaftsbury property as a wedding gift. Carol's interest in becoming a farmer pleased his father, who commented, "I always dreamed of being a real farmer: and seeing [Carol] one is almost the same as being one myself. My heart's in it with him."

Although Frost returned to Amherst to begin the second year of his contract in the fall of 1924, he knew that he would not stay. The University of Michigan had made an offer he could not refuse—a lifetime fellowship created just for him. He would have no teaching responsibilities, and the fellowship paid him $5,000 a year. He could have as much time as he wanted to write.

As he took this major step in his literary career, Frost received the good news of the birth of his first grandson, William Prescott Frost, on October 15, 1924. Celebrations continued with a fiftieth birthday party given for Frost by friends on March 26, 1925, at the Hotel Brevoort in New York City. One of Frost's supporters, Amy Lowell, did not attend because of illness. The master of ceremonies read aloud her greetings, her last communication

Robert Frost in 1925. (Courtesy of Getty Images.)

with Frost. Out of spite, Frost refused to attend a party for her the following week. She died six weeks later.

During the spring of 1925, Elinor became quite ill from a nervous collapse. Doctors discovered that fifty-year-old Elinor had suffered a miscarriage, perhaps brought on by her dread of moving to Michigan. Elinor found their pace of life more than she could bear. All the moves and constant visitors, especially students, were daunting. Knowing her husband's love of an almost constant open house, Elinor feared the social life on a larger campus. She wished that they could return to the Derry farm days when no one knew who Robert Frost was. She also did not like to be so far from her children, but Elinor never told Frost how she felt.

In August the Frosts accepted an invitation to spend the month at a cottage in the mountains. This sojourn removed them from the hay fever that bothered Frost each year, and the couple enjoyed a peaceful month before leaving for Michigan. Frost, intent on writing as much as possible, still had a hard time turning down all the invitations to speak and read his poetry, largely because he was still financially supporting his adult children.

After a hectic two-week tour in New Hampshire, New York, and North Carolina, Frost returned to Ann Arbor so exhausted that he collapsed from a case of severe influenza. After coming home, Frost always had a let-down that prevented him from getting any writing done. Elinor hated his public performances, and his barding around was a constant source of marital conflict. Elinor told Lesley, "Your father *must* give this up. His health is failing. His life is being ruined. His poetry is suffering. It *can't* go on."

Added to this conflict were the children's problems. Carol had inherited the family lung weakness, and Frost paid for his son to go to a higher, drier climate in Colorado. His daughter Marjorie suffered from chronic anxiety. When her condition worsened, Elinor went to Pittsfield to care for her. Frost missed Elinor and stopped keeping any kind of schedule while she was gone. He often slept until early afternoon and then stayed up most of the night. However, he had always been at his most creative after midnight, and he wrote several poems, such as "Spring Pools" and "A Winter Eden," during this period. They all contained New England imagery, even though Frost lived and wrote in Michigan. He said, "I never write about a place in New England, if I am there. I always write about it when I am away."

But Frost was not destined to settle in Michigan. After he had been there a year, the new president at Amherst, George Olds, came to visit Frost. He offered Frost a full professorship of English at a salary of $5,000 for ten weeks of teaching. Although the offer was financially weaker than Michigan's, Frost liked the eastern climate better, and he would be closer to his little grandson. He accepted the offer, brushing off any hard feelings that Michigan may have had about his abrupt departure, once again dodging his commitments and uprooting his family.

It is difficult to say whether family stress detracted

from Frost's professional goals, or, with all the moving around the country, those goals induced stress. His daughter-in-law Lillian needed surgery for a tubal pregnancy that almost killed her. Irma announced her plans to marry John Paine Cone and move to his family farm in Kansas. Elinor tried to cope with family illness and wedding plans but felt overwhelmed. All the activity made Frost nervous, and he could not write.

In January 1927 Frost began his ten weeks of teaching at Amherst, where he became quite popular. A student at the time later recalled Frost's visit to an afternoon German philosophy seminar:

> Frost began to discuss metaphors in an easy way, asking occasional questions to bring out our ideas. Gradually the evening shadows lengthened and after a while Frost alone was talking. The room grew darker and darker until we could not see each others' faces. But no one even thought of turning on the light. The dinner hour came and went, and still no one of that half score of hungry boys dreamed of leaving. We dared not even stir for fear of interrupting. Finally, long after seven, Frost stopped and said, 'Well, I guess that's enough.' We thanked him and left as if under a spell.

While at Amherst, Frost continued to gather the thirty-nine poems for his next collection, *West-Running Brook*. The book combined new poems and some so old that they could have appeared in *A Boy's Will*. The new title came from Frost's memory of a brook on the Derry farm that ran westward despite the fact that it must eventually empty into the Atlantic Ocean to the east. This brook that refused to flow in the right direction symbolized the individualism expressed in many of Frost's poems. Frost explored a variety of contrasts in life and nature, such as man's place in the universe, his struggle with nature, vocation and avocation, and man's spiritual nature versus his quest for scientific knowledge. Some of the poems required the work to be read in an ironic tone that, if not applied, changed the entire meaning. Only careful readers found the complex messages that Frost buried underneath metaphor, irony, and symbolism.

With the book ready for publication, Frost felt that he could now negotiate better terms with his publisher Holt. They agreed to publish *West-Running Brook* in fall 1928 and to have Frost's favorite illustrator, J. J. Lankes, do the woodcut illustrations. Holt promised to pay Frost $250 per month for the next five years as well as a $2,000 advance on royalties for the book, which would be 5 percent higher than those on his previous book. They also agreed to reprint *Selected Poems* and, within the next two years, publish *Collected Poems*.

Frost was fiercely jealous of attention going to someone other than him and worried about some of the modern poets whom he considered rivals—Edna St. Vincent Millay, Edwin Arlington Robinson, Vachel Lindsay, Edgar Lee Masters, and Carl Sandburg. Having been ignored so long in his own country, Frost did not want to yield the spotlight, even temporarily. However, his own reputation was solidified with the announcement of

The frontispiece for Frost's West-Running Brook *was a woodcut by J. J. Lankes.* (University of Virginia)

his second Pulitzer Prize for *Collected Poems* and with his election to the American Academy of Arts and Letters in 1930.

All of this success allowed Frost to escape the economic distress of the Great Depression. Though massive unemployment, bankruptcies, bread lines, and suicides resulted from the collapse of the United States' economy, Frost remained seemingly untouched.

Once again, family issues dampened Frost's success. Marjorie and daughter-in-law Lillian both caught tuberculosis. The children moved west to take advantage of a better climate, and Robert and Elinor traveled with them. On top of that, Lesley's marriage suffered from her husband's infidelities.

Back east, on November 16, 1932, Frost attended a dinner honoring American poet T. S. Eliot. The two had first met in London at Harold Monro's Poetry Bookshop, when they both lived in England. At their first meeting, the two strangers exchanged barbs about each other's writing. Eliot believed that poetry had to be difficult in order to engage the reader in its meaning. Before he met Frost for the first time, Eliot had written in an article: "His verse, it is regretfully said, is uninteresting, and

Modernist poet T. S. Eliot was born in St. Louis, Missouri, but spent most of his life living as an expatriate in England. (National Portrait Gallery, London)

what is uninteresting is unreadable, and what is unreadable is not read." Frost had responded on numerous occasions on the lecture circuit by criticizing Eliot's pretentious scholarship. At that first meeting in England, Frost also took offense at Eliot's assumed British accent and his superior attitude.

At their second meeting at Harvard, Frost resented the way the faculty flattered Eliot. At the dinner's conclusion, the host read a few of Eliot's poems. Then someone suggested that both Eliot and Frost read a recent poem of their own. Eliot replied, "I will if Frost will." Frost declined. He used the excuse that he had just published *Collected Poems* and did not have any new material ready.

When the other guests expressed their disappointment, Frost claimed that he would write an entirely new poem while Eliot read. Frost pretended to write on the backs of place cards, but when he arose to read, it was obvious that he used a poem previously written. The deception led to an argument between the two poets about Robert Burns and other Scottish writers. Eliot had no use for any of them. Because of his mother's Scottish background, Frost felt compelled to defend them. Eliot's remarks offended Frost, and their relationship remained strained for many years.

After Marjorie recovered from tuberculosis, she met and married a man named Willard Fraser in 1933. Marjorie was soon pregnant. Though her child was healthy, Marjorie became ill with puerperal fever and died on May 2, 1934.

Two weeks later, Frost wrote to his friend Louis Untermeyer: "The noblest of us all is dead and has taken our hearts out of the world with her." Since Lillian had recovered from tuberculosis, she and Carol kept Marjorie's daughter Robin for several months each year so that the child could know her mother's family. However, the moves back and forth gradually exhausted everyone, and Robin finally stayed in Montana to be raised by her father and her grandmother, Willard's mother.

The many trips and the emotional stress took their toll on Elinor, who suffered a heart attack in November 1934. As soon as Elinor was strong enough to travel, doctors recommended that she spend the winter in Florida. The warmer climate would benefit not only her but Frost. Their daughter-in-law Lillian's doctor said that the climate would be good for her as well. They all decided to go to Key West, where they located two rental houses close to each other. Frost found Key West a strange place, but the only thing that really bothered him was the fact that the city was the site of one of President Franklin D. Roosevelt's New Deal projects designed to help the nation out of the Great Depression. The politically conservative Frost, with his individualistic beliefs, resented such activities of the federal government, equating the New Deal with Soviet communism. Frost opposed any kind of collective action, including a minimum wage, labor unions, social security, and medical insurance. He supported self-reliance and believed that a man's first duty was to protect himself. This appears

Key West, originally colonized by the Spanish in 1521, became a popular retreat for writers in the early twentieth century. In addition to Frost, famous literati residents have included Tennessee Williams, Wallace Stevens, Elizabeth Bishop, Ernest Hemingway, and James Merrill. (Library of Congress)

to be something of a contradiction for Frost, as he had once depended so much upon the support of his grandfather and his inheritance. Elinor encouraged him in these conservative beliefs, and Frost wrote long letters of complaint to Louis Untermeyer, whom he knew supported the president's efforts to bring the country out of the Great Depression.

That summer, back in New England, Frost wrote the introduction to *King Jaspar*, the last volume of poetry by his friend Edwin Arlington Robinson, who had recently died. Writing the introduction gave Frost the opportunity to express his opinions about modern poetry. He wrote, "It may come to the notice of posterity (and then again it may not) that this our age ran wild in the quest of new ways to be new." He mentioned various attempts authors made to seem original by omitting punctuation, capital letters, meter, and images. He concluded by wondering where the originality was in that.

Frost attended the Rocky Mountain Writers' Conference and spoke to overflowing crowds in the largest auditorium available. Humorous and engaging, Frost used his own unique way to speak of doctrines in which he strongly believed. Frost asserted that when the goodness of life was measured by material values, mankind moved further and further away from nature, the chief subject of art.

When he finally returned to New England in August 1935, Frost began to think about another book. As he looked at his poems, he was surprised at how many he had. Although he had published individual poems in magazines, he had not published a volume since 1928. Frost began work on his next collection, *A Further Range*.

The word "range" had several different meanings to the poet—the Green Mountains in Vermont where the Frosts now lived, a new range of poems with political themes, and a range of genres, including animal fable, ballad, comedy, dramatic monologue, epigram, historical narrative, lyric, satire, and wedding song. In this collection, Frost extended the political and religious explorations begun in *New Hampshire*, but this time he spoke more directly to the reader in a morally instructive manner. Frost reiterated previous stances on individual rights and spoke out against workers acting together to resolve industrial disputes. Despite his own association

The beautiful Green Mountains of Vermont provided a powerful backdrop for Frost's poetry in the 1930s. (Library of Congress)

with many universities, Frost ridiculed the mindless bureaucracy of academic departments.

The theme of individualism continued to dominate many of his poems in response to the economic and social difficulties of the Great Depression. To make his point, Frost frequently turned to satire in addressing the vices, foolishness, and abuses of the government. In "Provide, Provide," Frost warned readers to provide for themselves, even if it meant buying friends, in order to avoid government care:

> Die early and avoid the fate.
> Or if predestined to die late,
> Make up your mind to die in state.
>
> . . .
>
> Better to go down dignified
> With boughten friendship at your side
> Than none at all. Provide, provide!

In the spring of 1936, Frost delivered the Charles Eliot Norton lectures at Harvard. Frost titled the six-lecture series "The Renewal of Words," an apt title because the lectures were renewals of previous addresses. The first lecture, "The Old Way to Be New," was a reworking of the introduction Frost wrote for Robinson's *King Jaspar*. The only difference was that Frost used his own poems to illustrate the points. The second was a summation of all Frost had said in the past twenty years about the sound of sense, while the other four lectures touched on other familiar viewpoints. Nevertheless, the talks drew huge crowds. A reporter for the *Boston Herald* wrote that Frost conveyed "the importance of poetry as speech that was somehow essential, and when he recited lines of verse, his own or that of other poets, you understood exactly what he meant. He had a way of 'saying' a poem that struck you between the eyes, and in the heart. The audience was appropriately dazzled."

The university planned to publish the lectures at their conclusion, but Frost never wrote any of his talks, and he did not know how he was going to give them the copies they wanted. He tried to solve the problem by hiring a stenographer to attend the lectures and write down what he said. However, Frost never delivered a final copy to the Harvard University Press. Reading the stenographer's transcription, he realized that his "off-the-cuff," rambling style lost its effectiveness when formally written.

At the conclusion of the lecture series, several of

Frost's friends who taught at Harvard wanted Frost to join them on the faculty. One of the professors, Theodore Morrison, and his wife Kathleen, known as Kay, hosted receptions after five of the six lectures. Kay had first met Frost when she was a student at Bryn Mawr and editor of the college newspaper. She was one of a small group of undergraduates who had arranged for Frost to teach the three-session writing course at Bryn Mawr. The Norton lecture series gave Frost and Kay a chance to renew their acquaintance.

The publication of *A Further Range* followed quickly on the heels of the lectures. And with Frost's renown and growing fame, he achieved a new milestone with the collection. The Book-of-the-Month Club named it as a selection. That guaranteed the immediate sale of 50,000 copies, a significant number for a book of poetry, and strong royalty payments. Still, Frost anxiously awaited reviews.

He did not have to wait long for the reaction. Several reviews criticized the work because of Frost's increasingly conservative political views. Critics claimed that Frost was out of touch with the times. However, the review that sent Frost into depression appeared in *The New England Quarterly:*

> The voice is still the voice of Frost, it is true, and all the tricks are here; but the diction is faded, the expression imprecise, and the tone extraordinarily tired and uneasy. It is a strange thing that Robert Frost, pondering the

problem of a sick society, should suddenly become ineffectual, should seem unable to deal abstractly with matter that he has powerfully suggested in many of his best lyrics.

Although Louis Untermeyer and other friends wrote positive reviews of *A Further Range*, Frost withdrew from public scrutiny. He cancelled lectures and readings. When he had delivered the Norton lectures at Harvard in the spring, he had also made arrangements to move his Amherst teaching to the fall, but he cancelled that as well. For the first time since returning to America, his professional life rivaled his private life for sadness.

Then suddenly a flurry of positive reviews appeared in opposition to the negative ones printed earlier. A review in the London *Sunday Times* showed that he was still appreciated in England: "Mr. Frost now occupies in his own land the position which Mr. [William Butler] Yeats now occupies in ours. . . . More than any other American poet [Frost] is securely in the tradition of English verse."

About the same time, Holt published a collection of essays about Frost and his work called *Recognition of Robert Frost: Twenty-Fifth Anniversary*. These essays all praised Frost, the poet. The value of *A Further Range* was confirmed in May 1937 when Frost received his third Pulitzer Prize for it. In June Harvard added to the accolades by awarding Frost an honorary doctor of letters.

However, all the recognition could not soften the greatest sorrow of his life. In December Frost and Elinor went to Gainesville, Florida. This time they decided to buy a house so that they would always have a place to stay. Returning from looking at real estate one day in March, Elinor suffered a severe heart attack as she went up the apartment stairs. In the next two days, she had seven more attacks. On March 20, 1938, Frost's wife of forty-three years died.

The tragedy overwhelmed Frost, and he became ill as well. He worried that he had been responsible for her death by keeping such a hectic travel schedule and encouraging a large family. He wanted to ask her forgiveness, but he missed the chance to talk with her during her final hours.

Lesley and a friend took Elinor's body to Jacksonville for cremation, but the memorial service was postponed because of Frost's illness. His family showed little support. Frost asked Lesley if he could live with her. Still distraught over the death of her mother, she said no. Lesley, who had witnessed Robert's late-night threat to kill himself or her mother, blamed him for her mother's death. These accusations hurt Frost deeply. In an August letter to his illustrator, J. J. Lankes, Frost confessed, "I'm afraid I dragged [Elinor] through pretty much of a life for one as frail as she was. Too many children, too many habitations, too many vicissitudes. And a faith required that would have exhausted most women."

Frost recognized that the future would be rough, and

he wrote to his friend Benny DeVoto, "I shall be all right in public, but I can't tell you how I am going to behave when I am alone. . . . I am going to work very hard . . . and be on the go with people so as not to try myself solitary too soon." The life of a poet was already lonely business, and Frost couldn't bear any more of it by himself.

seven

A Man with Friends

Frost's days passed slowly without Elinor. He had dedicated most of his poems and, until her death, all of his books to her. Many friends offered to help him through this difficult time. The president of Amherst came to Florida to comfort Frost and helped to make arrangements for a memorial service at the college's Johnson Chapel. The ceremony, held in April 1938, ended Frost's formal ties to Amherst. He could not bear to live in the house that he and Elinor had occupied, so he offered his resignation.

Elinor's wish was to have her ashes scattered among the alder trees along Hyla Brook on the Derry farm. After he sold their house and concluded his business at Amherst, Frost went to the Derry farm. He approached it with mixed emotions. He wanted to enjoy the memories there yet dreaded them also. So many images from the farm had found their way into his poetry, and in his mind's eye he still retained those pictures. But the Derry farm had been neglected and Frost found he could not scatter Elinor's ashes without believing it would dishonor her memory. He returned to South Shaftsbury, Vermont, where he lived with Carol and his family. He kept Elinor's ashes in a large cupboard in his bedroom there.

Frost tried to resume a normal life but found he always needed people around him. He spent hours talking to Carol, Lillian, and his grandson Prescott, now fourteen years old. He was convinced that he could never live alone because he had always depended on Elinor to help him deal with loneliness. As he later told an interviewer, he spent the rest of his life fighting loneliness by constantly surrounding himself with friends and family. He went so far as to make sure he had someone to talk to at night to help him fall asleep.

Without having to teach at Amherst, Frost was free to write. But thoughts would not come. He did not know and did not care if he could ever again write a good poem. As he wandered around the farm, his thoughts bordered on insanity as he blamed himself for his wife's death. At such times he wished his ashes could join Elinor's inside the urn.

In July, Frost received a visit from an old friend, Kathleen (Kay) Morrison. Kay was the wife of Theodore (Ted) Morrison, a supporter during the Charles Eliot Norton lectures at Harvard. She had come to Vermont to see some friends. While she was there, she decided to stop by South Shaftsbury to see how Frost was doing. Appalled at his emotional state, she invited him to spend some time with her and her children, Robert and Anne, at the house where they were vacationing.

At the time, Frost was sixty-four years old but still energetic and handsome despite his snow-white hair. The thirty-nine-year-old, auburn-haired Kay was pretty, polished, and well dressed. Within a short time, Frost became infatuated with her. Until Elinor's death Frost had never had a relationship with another woman. Rashly, he asked her to divorce Ted and marry him.

Kay explained to Frost that she was happily married and would never consider divorce because of the effect it would have on her two children. Frost and Kay's relationship created a strange triangle with Ted. Although he obviously knew of their interest in each other, Ted, who served as director of the Bread Loaf Writers' Conference in Vermont, invited Frost to lecture there in August. Frost gave an excellent presentation that led to his having a major role in future Bread Loaf meetings. At the conclusion of the session, Frost expressed his gratitude to the Morrisons: "You two rescued me from a very dangerous self when you had the idea of keeping me for the whole session at Bread Loaf. . . . I came away from you as good as saved. I had had a long lovers' quarrel with the world. I loved the world, but you might never have guessed it from the things I thought and said. Now the quarrel is made up."

Frost at Bread Loaf in August, 1938.

Soon, Kay and Frost began a years-long affair. Kay tried to keep both her husband and Frost content by telling each that she did not have sexual relations with the other. Frost believed that this called into question his manhood and told several close friends about the affair despite Kay's appeal to keep their liaison secret. In later years, Frost encouraged biographers to include the story. He believed that the full story of his relationship with Kay was necessary for a complete understanding of his life and work. Publicly, Kay denied the relationship by saying that Frost was an old man who had sexual fantasies and that she was just his secretary who answered correspondence and arranged his lecture schedule.

Frost planned to move to Boston to be nearer to Kay, who had quit her part-time job as a reader for The Atlantic Monthly Press to function as a secretary for Frost. He became ill with respiratory problems and spent part of September 1938 in Massachusetts General Hospital in Boston. After he released himself without a doctor's permission, Kay found Frost an apartment that he could use as a base from which to travel to his lectures and poetry readings.

At the end of November, Frost delivered an afternoon lecture at Harvard University. Officials there believed that a presentation by one of their former Charles Norton lecturers would attract a few hundred people at best, and assigned him a room of that size. More than a thousand people came to hear him. The large group pleased Frost as well as the "Friends of

Robert Frost," a group of Harvard alumni who were trying to raise $4,000 to secure a two-year appointment for Frost at the university.

Shortly after his appearance at Harvard, Frost renegotiated his contract with Henry Holt and Company and received some of the most generous terms ever offered a writer. In doing so, he also agreed to write a preface for a new edition of his *Collected Poems*. In the introduction, Frost described the "figure" of a poem: "it begins in delight and ends in wisdom."

With winter approaching, Frost planned to head south once again, but he didn't get far before receiving notice that the National Institute of Arts had awarded him its Gold Medal for "distinguished work in poetry." The Institute president would present the award at a dinner on January 18, 1939. Only three times prior to Frost's award had the Gold Medal gone to a poet.

Following his winter in Florida, Frost received a letter from the Harvard University president, inviting Frost to become the Ralph Waldo Emerson Fellow in Poetry. After the success of Frost's Norton lectures at Harvard, his supporters had convinced the president to offer a two-year appointment at an annual salary of $1,500 paid for by the "Friends of Robert Frost." Although Frost was not sure that he wanted to align himself with a particular university again, he did not want to disappoint the people who had worked so hard on his behalf. According to the terms of the agreement, Frost had no formal duties but would hopefully meet with students occasionally and from time to time give public lectures. Frost decided to accept the fellowship.

That summer Frost returned to the Bread Loaf Writers' Conference. He decided to buy a house so that he would have a place to stay each time he taught there. He found the Herman Noble farm in Ripton, Vermont, just two miles from the campus. The property contained a farmhouse and a cottage, open fields, and a mountain view. It became his permanent summer residence.

Trying to balance his need for privacy with his need to associate with people, Frost invited the Morrisons to share the property. Kay and Ted lived in the farmhouse,

Frost (far right) *visits with Kay and Ted Morrison at the Bread Loaf Writers' Conference.* (Courtesy of Dartmouth College Library.)

and Frost in the cottage. Kay cooked meals for all of them. She and Frost spoke via telephone when he felt the need for company. Ted seemed willing to put up with the unusual arrangement in order to avoid a public acknowledgement of Kay's unfaithfulness.

In the fall of 1939, Frost began his fellowship at Harvard and taught one class on poetry. Before going to Florida for the winter, Frost decided to buy a permanent residence in Boston.

The money to buy another property came from Earle J. Bernheimer, a wealthy collector of Frost books. Bernheimer approached Frost about "renting" the little poetry volume called "Twilight" that Frost had printed for Elinor before they married. Frost had made only two copies, one of which he destroyed when Elinor did not seem impressed by the slender volume. Bernheimer's proposal was to rent the book and display it as a part of his collection. When Bernheimer died, the book would be willed to a library of Frost's choice.

At first, Frost was uncertain about trusting Bernheimer. He finally told Bernheimer that the rental cost was $1,000 to each of Frost's children. Bernheimer agreed and relieved Frost of some of the financial burden of his adult children who never outgrew their dependency upon their parents. His own desire to protect his children from the poverty he had known as a child was a definite factor in this continued support.

Kay Morrison and her son Bobby accompanied Frost to Florida, where he would eventually be met by his official biographer, Lawrance Thompson, a Princeton University professor. Since Frost was not strong enough to look for a house, they stayed at Casa Marina, a hotel in Key West. There Frost met Hyde Cox, a Harvard graduate who had attended all of Frost's Norton lectures. Despite the fact that Cox was in his twenties, the two men had shared many experiences. They discussed these during the frequent long walks that Frost took to regain his strength. Gradually, a strong friendship developed, and Cox became almost like a son to Frost.

Frost bought five acres of undeveloped pine land in Coconut Grove and built two small pre-fabricated houses that he named Pencil Pines. His son Carol still wanted to move permanently to Florida, and Frost had initially hoped that Carol could oversee the construction. But Carol had become increasingly fearful and paranoid, apparently the next Frost to suffer from mental illness. He believed that his New England neighbors plotted against him. When he learned that his wife Lillian needed surgery, Carol became irrationally fearful that she would die and leave him to care for their teenage son Prescott. Several times Carol mentioned suicide, and with his unstable mental condition, Lillian asked Frost to come stay at their house while she was in the hospital.

Since childhood Carol had been withdrawn and un-sociable. He had few friends and thus had become extremely close to his mother. Her death rocked the foundation of his life. Carol knew few successes in life and felt inferior in comparison to his successful father.

Frost's perpetual financial support, plus his attempts to guide his son, led to Carol's further feelings of failure. Although Carol's marriage to Lillian had been good for him, it also increased his responsibilities. Lillian's deafness further contributed to Carol's sense of isolation. But Carol never admitted any weakness or illness. Even when his symptoms became serious, he refused to recognize them as mental illness.

Frost came to South Shaftsbury, where he had long conversations with his son. He tried to convince Carol that he had much to live for. After several days, Frost decided that Carol had regained his mental stability. On October 8, 1940, Frost traveled to Ripton, Vermont. The next morning at 7 AM his grandson Prescott called Frost to tell him that Carol had killed himself with a deer rifle. The shot woke Prescott, who discovered his father on the kitchen floor, with a bullet wound in his head. Prescott called the police, Frost, and a family friend. The boy's calm handling of the situation earned praise from his grandfather, who told him, "Disaster brought out the heroic in you. You now know you have the courage and nerve for anything you may want or need to be. . . . You would have had plenty of excuse if you had gone to pieces and run out of that house crying for help."

Frost delivered the sad news to Lillian, who was still in the hospital after nearly dying following her surgery. There were many reasons for Carol's suicide, but Frost blamed himself. To his friend Louis Untermeyer, Frost wrote, "I took the wrong way with [Carol]. I tried many ways and every single one of them was wrong. Some thing in me is still asking for the chance to try one more. There's where the greatest pain is located. I am cut off too abruptly in my plans and efforts for his peace of mind." In just six years, Frost had suffered the deaths of three beloved family members—Marjorie, Elinor, and Carol.

Frost still had one more sad duty to perform—final placement of the ashes of both his wife and his son. Frost purchased a large piece of land in the cemetery in Bennington's Old First Congregational Church in the shadow of the Green Mountains of Vermont. He planned

The Old First Congregational Church in Bennington, Vermont, where many members of the Frost family are buried, eventually including Robert Frost himself.

to use it as a burial ground for all of the Frosts. With Lillian's approval, he made arrangements to have two recesses dug and stones made bearing the names of the deceased. On a September day, Frost, Lillian, and his grandson Prescott interred the urns containing the ashes of their loved ones. As he aged, the innate sadness Frost had known all his life became much more vivid.

eight

Poet-in-Residence

In the twenty-six years since Robert Frost had returned home from his time in England, he had come to be considered a truly American poet. While he had witnessed World War I, the Great Depression, and many changes of the early twentieth century, he continued to work the same inward-looking themes.

In March 1941, he traveled to Washington, DC, where his work was the second exhibition in a series featuring American poets at the Library of Congress. Reporters praised his speech, "The Role of a Poet in Democracy," in which he focused on the Great Seal of the United States—a pyramid with an eye at its apex. Frost said that, like poetry, it was a symbol, one signifying that "democracy would always mean refraining from power beyond a certain point; that we would never in this country have anybody at the apex but God"—the all-seeing eye at the pyramid's peak. This speech added to Frost's reputation as a national poet. In the fall, Harvard University invited him to accept a position as a fellow of American civilization. This appointment provided a way for Harvard to keep Frost on campus after the expiration of his initial two-year fellowship. As before, the position required little of Frost. He was to act as a consultant in history and literature for an annual salary of $3,000.

On December 5, 1941, Frost served as the Phi Beta Kappa poet, sponsored by the country's most prestigious honor society, at a ceremony at the College of William and Mary. For the occasion he read a poem written in 1935 but never before presented publicly. "The Gift Outright" celebrated America's development into a nation after separation from England:

> The land was ours before we were the land's.
> She was our land more than a hundred years
> Before we were her people.

Just two days after Frost celebrated America, the Japanese bombed Pearl Harbor. Although Frost generally supported war, this time he criticized President Roosevelt for getting the United States involved in a war for which it was not prepared. He further accused England of joining a war it could not handle and then drawing the United States into the battle to help.

Frost's bitter remarks reflected not only opposition to the government but also a fear of what war would do to his income. He believed that he would receive fewer lecture invitations, and he depended on that money to take care of family obligations. Frost turned to collector Earle J. Bernheimer, who had previously rented "Twilight." The two reached an agreement that Frost would regularly send literary documents, such as original drafts of poems, to Bernheimer, who would pay Frost $150 a month regardless of what collectibles he received during that period. Despite this arrangement, Frost's financial fears did not go away. His friend Rabbi Victor Reichert revealed: "There was never enough [money], in his mind. He remained suspicious of the future, and was perpetually anticipating some dire event that would wipe him out financially."

Frost began work on a new volume of poetry, *A Witness Tree*. Although he feared it might not sell in a wartime economy, his publisher assured him that Americans valued all things that were their own. Since Frost's poetry fit into that category, they predicted advance sales of 7,500 copies of *A Witness Tree*, which Frost dedicated to Kay Morrison. For the volume Frost selected poems from as far back as 1896 and as recent as ones that he had just written. Frost's style had not changed significantly, so poems from early and late in his career intermingled easily. He divided the forty-two poems into five sections that moved from a look at the human soul's isolation and need for love to the larger world and political commentary.

The book also reflected Frost's strong interest in

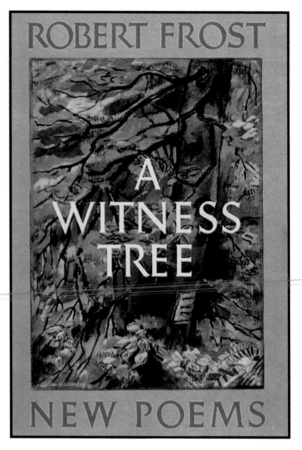

Published in 1942, A Witness Tree *included Frost's famous poem "The Gift Outright," as well as many other poems, such as "Never Again Would Birds' Song Be the Same," that continue to be taught and studied in schools.* (University of Virginia)

geology, archeology, and astronomy—sciences that led him to a less human-centered view of the natural world, as illustrated in "Our Hold on the Planet":

> There is much in nature against us. But we forget:
> Take nature altogether since time began,
> Including human nature, in peace and war.

And it must be a little more in favor of man,
Say a fraction of one percent at the very least,
Or our number living wouldn't be steadily more,
Our hold on the planet wouldn't have so increased.

Critics loved the book. "His writing is clearer, more pointed, simpler, and richer than it ever has been," proclaimed a reviewer in *Current History*. Writer Stephen Vincent Benet commented, "This is a beautiful book, serene, observing, and passionate." By mid-June the publisher had sold over 10,000 copies, and more orders streamed in. Along with this outpouring of praise appeared the first full-length critical study of Frost's work, *Fire and Ice: The Art and Thought of Robert Frost*, by Lawrance Thompson.

This validation of him as a poet alleviated some of Frost's financial fears, and he began to alter his stance against the war. With the enlistment of his grandson Prescott, his son-in-law Willard Fraser, and his biographer Lawrance Thompson, Frost could no longer condemn America's fight. Frost hoped that if his grandson had an interest in the military, he would try for an appointment to West Point. However, the eighteen-year-old Prescott followed his own desires and enlisted in the Army Signal Corps.

Frost had begun to feel that his fellowship at Harvard did not provide the kind of relationship he wanted with a university. Before he could even look around for a different placement, Dartmouth University, where he had once been a student for a part of a semester, offered him a position as the George Ticknor Fellow for the Humanities at a salary of $3,000 per year. Another attraction to the offer was that his friend Sidney Cox taught in the Dartmouth English department.

In May Frost received word that *A Witness Tree* had won the 1942 Pulitzer Prize for poetry. Although the prize committee hesitated to give Frost the award for the fourth time, Frost's friend Louis Untermeyer urged them to do so. However, the committee, whose decision was not final, recommended another poet to the Columbia Board of Trustees, which controlled the Pulitzer awards. Untermeyer wrote a dissenting report to the trustees. He urged them not to overlook the best volume of poetry just because its author had received previous awards. The board of trustees agreed with Untermeyer and named Frost the winner.

It was not the first time Frost's friendships had worked to his advantage. He had fostered relationships with several board members of the Book-of-the-Month Club, which helped secure *A Further Range* as a club selection, a lucrative reward.

In October 1943, Frost began his fellowship at Dartmouth. In this new role, he met with students from Friday to Sunday in the fall and spring. He gave occasional lectures and appeared at ceremonies, including graduation. The lax schedule allowed Frost to spend time with Kay in Boston, Mondays through Wednesdays. Although Frost had a good first semester, pneumonia

Frost converses with a group of engrossed students during his fellowship years at Dartmouth in the 1940s. (Courtesy of Dartmouth College Library.)

caused him to spend Christmas in the Dartmouth infirmary.

Frost's recovery was slower than anticipated, and he worried that he might be unable to meet the commitments of his spring lecture schedule.

Frost faced another problem. His longtime friend Louis Untermeyer was editing Office of War Information publications. He urged Frost to write propaganda for the agency. With his strong sense of independence and individualism, Frost preferred to remain separate from any organized war effort. But as Hitler's campaign against the Jews in Europe accelerated, Untermeyer, who was Jewish, made a personal appeal to Frost at the

Bread Loaf Writers' Conference in August 1944. When Frost refused to help, Untermeyer interpreted his refusal as a lack of concern for the Jews. Untermeyer left the conference and refused to respond to notes from Frost. Frost later wrote a long letter in verse form explaining that he just thought of Jews as Americans and not as a separate group. He concluded by saying that his greatest wish was to have all animosity end, especially that between him and his friend. Untermeyer felt Frost was sincere, and the rift was mended.

In March 1945, Frost published a short play that he called *A Masque of Reason.* Many saw the drama, based on the Biblical sufferings of Job, as Frost's way of trying to deal with the deaths of Elinor, Carol, and Marjorie. Critics did not receive the drama with much enthusiasm. A review in *The New Yorker* said, "Frost, bringing us up against the problem of Pain and Evil, adds nothing to our insight on the subject." Despite the attacks on his first masque, Frost later wrote a second one based on the Biblical story of Jonah and the whale. He called the work *A Masque of Mercy.* This drama received even harsher criticism, with one reviewer calling it "a bad book, shallow, corny, and unmercifully cute." Ignoring the critics, Frost talked to a Broadway producer about performing the two short plays back-to-back, but the producer did not see the material as appropriate for Broadway.

In the fall of 1945 Frost began his third year as Ticknor Fellow at Dartmouth. He was seventy years old, and in many ways his life was better than it had been for a long time. Frost had more lecture invitations than he could fill, he had received four Pulitzer Prizes, he had a circle of friends in each of the places he resided, and his health had improved. With this rosy outlook, Frost began to collect poems for his next volume, *Steeple Bush*, planned for a 1947 publication date.

As usual, though, family problems eventually intruded. Irma and her husband John Cone divorced in 1946 after a two-year separation. Irma, like Frost's sister Jeanie, suffered from paranoia. Doctors predicted that she would be unable to live by herself much longer. After the divorce Irma wanted to come stay with Frost. Her youngest son, six-year-old Harold, lived with his mother, and Frost did not believe that he could tolerate having them in the house with him. He enlisted Kay's help and they found a house for Irma in nearby Acton.

Steeple Bush, Frost's eighth volume of verse and his first lyric collection in five years, was published in early 1947. The title referred to a plant that grew wild on his Ripton farm. Frost dedicated the book to his six grandchildren: Prescott (Carol's son), Jacky and Harold (Irma's sons), Elinor and Lesley Lee Ballantine (Lesley's daughters), and Robin (Marjorie's daughter).

Frost dreaded the reviews because he worried critics were looking for signs of declining creativity, but most critics treated Frost kindly. Reviewers all pointed to "Directive" as the outstanding offering in the forty-three-poem collection. The first four sections of *Steeple*

Bush explored the human condition in its various forms. But as he had done in several other volumes, Frost used the last section of the book to express his resentment at government interference and ineffectiveness.

One exception to the book's generally positive reception was a November 1947 review by the noted American poet-critic Randall Jarrell, whose stature as a critic had helped to establish the reputation of many poets. Previously, Jarrell had written several essays lauding Frost's work and had admitted Frost's influence on his own writing. Jarrell wrote, "Most of the poems merely remind you . . . that they are productions of somebody who once, and somewhere else, was a great poet." Because

National Book Award-winning poet and preeminent critic Randall Jarrell. (University of North Carolina at Greensboro)

of Jarrell's reputation and his past writings about Frost, this assessment, in particular, stung.

Jarrell later published an essay in which he stated that Frost's poems "begin with a flat and terrible reproduction of the evil in the world and end by saying: It's so; and there's nothing you can do about it." Jarrell called Frost the "subtlest and saddest of poets." He supported this description by discussing Frost's dominant themes of alienation, loneliness, and spiritual desolation. Jarrell claimed that it was lack of understanding of this side of Frost that caused intellectuals to ignore him.

Frost cared very much about his reviews, possibly too much given all the awards, publications, honors, and praise in his past. Kay Morrison tried very hard to keep negative reviews from him. If he found one, it had the power to send him into an emotional tailspin.

Shortly after Jarrell's disappointing review, Frost received a surprise visit from T. S. Eliot, whom he had not seen for over ten years. Eliot had come to the United States to visit an ill brother. To help with travel expenses, Eliot was giving the Charles Eliot Norton lectures at Harvard. He appeared to have no ill feelings toward Frost, even though he must have recalled their clash years before. Frost found Eliot a friendly, charming guest. As the two visited, they discussed the fate of Ezra Pound, the American poet living in England who had helped Frost with reviews of his earliest poetry. Pound had been arrested and declared insane for making treasonous wartime broadcasts on Rome radio. He was now in St. Elizabeth's Hospital, an institution for the criminally insane in Washington, DC.

Pound's fate was a sadly familiar one to the Frost family. Just as he had been forced to commit his sister Jeanie to an institution in 1920, Frost had to do the same for his daughter Irma in the summer of 1948. It was an extremely difficult decision, but Frost could not see an alternative. A few days after leaving her at the state hospital in Concord, New Hampshire, Frost wrote to Louis Untermeyer: "Cast your eye back over my family luck and perhaps you will wonder if I haven't had pretty near enough."

nine

Quilt of Honors

Over the years, the collector Earle Bernheimer had assembled an extensive collection of Frost's original memorabilia. Frost had helped him do so with the hope that some day it would all go to a university library. Although Frost knew that Bernheimer had been involved in a lengthy and expensive divorce and child-custody suit, he did not realize how costly it was until he visited Bernheimer in California. At that time, Bernheimer indicated he might try to sell "Twilight," the rented volume that he now considered his possession. He believed that because of Frost's rising reputation, the book would bring twice the $4,000 Bernheimer had paid for it. He further upset Frost by saying that if he could not sell the entire collection to a library, he would auction the individual pieces to other collectors. Frost breathed a sigh of relief when Bernheimer took no immediate steps to sell anything.

Early in February 1948, Frost received a letter from Charles Cole, president of Amherst College, informing Frost that the board of trustees had voted to confer on him an honorary doctorate of letters degree at the spring graduation. Although Frost no longer had an official relationship with Amherst, he hoped that the degree might be a first step toward the college's inviting him back to its faculty. In June, Frost accepted the degree and then went back to Dartmouth in the fall to begin his fifth year there.

During this final tenure, Frost gave a lecture for the "Great Issues" course established by President John Dickey in 1947 as a requirement for all graduating seniors. Frost told the young men (Dartmouth did not admit women until 1973) that it was important for them to form opinions. Otherwise, there is no basis for conversation with those who agree or disagree. The importance of having and holding such ideas he called "some obstinacy," the title that he gave to his lecture. His talk touched on such diverse subjects as space exploration, treason, and the two sides of man— scientific and spiritual.

In November, Frost received an invitation from Amherst's president to return as the Simpson Lecturer in Literature with minimal responsibilities. By the time Frost concluded negotiations with Cole, he had a five-year contract at $3,500 a year and, for the first

time ever, the promise of an annual retirement payment of $2,500.

By this time, Frost's writing had slowed to a trickle.
Each Christmas he printed a few poems in small booklets
that he sent to friends. In 1949, Holt issued a new volume
called *The Complete Poems of Robert Frost*. The
clothbound edition included all of the poems from *A
Boy's Will* in 1913 to *Steeple Bush* in 1947. A *Time*
magazine cover story read: "Of living U.S. poets, none
has lodged poems more surely where they will be hard
to get rid of." This was actually a play on Frost's own
words, in which he once stated that his goal as a poet was
"to lodge a few pebbles where they will be hard to get
rid of." The *Time* cover featured Frost as a strong, rugged
New England man. The truth, however, was that Frost
still suffered from depression caused by the physical
strain of his lecture tours and the constant internal battle
between his need for privacy and his need to be with
people. The new book secured his reputation as a poet
once and for all, and early in 1950, Frost received word
that he was under consideration for the Nobel Prize for
Literature.

However, the committee gave the award to Britain's
Bertrand Russell. The ultimate literary prize would continue to elude Frost for the rest of his life. Since his
poems were based upon the peculiarities of common
New England speech, translation into other languages
destroyed their meaning. This may have accounted for
his being passed over not only this time but several times

Robert Frost was one of very few poets to be featured on the cover of Time *magazine. (Courtesy of Getty Images.)*

afterward. To offset the Nobel snub, the United States Senate passed a resolution to bring greetings to Frost on the occasion of his seventy-fifth birthday on March 26, 1950. Actually, they were a year late, as an earlier public document had reported Frost's birth year as 1875 instead of 1874, a mistake that had persisted for some time.

During the same year, Frost saw the books and manuscripts collected by Earle Bernheimer go on the auction block. Frost had feared this since first learning about Bernheimer's financial problems. Bernheimer offered all that he had for $18,000.

Frost told Bernheimer in numerous letters that "the sale of the collection will give me no offence." But as soon as he realized that no single buyer was coming forward and that the collection was going to be split up, Frost began to speak out against Bernheimer, whom he accused of betrayal. Many of Frost's friends sympathized with his position, and the bids remained low in order not to reward Bernheimer. The auction brought in only $14,695, and "Twilight," for which Bernheimer had paid $4,000, sold for only $3,500 at auction. Nevertheless, according to a *New York Times Book Review*, it was "reportedly the highest price ever paid for a single work by an American author."

Ironically, as his poetic output declined, Frost's reputation expanded. He accepted his twenty-fifth honorary degree at the University of North Carolina at Chapel Hill in June 1953. In August, the Academy of American Poets awarded him a $5,000 prize. For Frost's eightieth birthday, his publisher, Holt and Company, held a dinner at New York's Waldorf-Astoria Hotel for eighty guests, including senators, judges, writers, and critics.

Frost traveled to Brazil, Israel, and England as a goodwill ambassador for the United States. While in Great Britain, he received honorary degrees from Oxford and Cambridge universities. After accepting yet another honorary degree, this one from Dartmouth, Frost had all the doctoral hoods he had received made into a quilt. He had moved beyond being just a writer. He was a literary icon.

By that time, Frost's reputation was such that poet Archibald MacLeish sought his help in freeing Ezra Pound from St. Elizabeth's Hospital in Washington. Frost had long resented Pound for the peremptory review of *North of Boston* that Pound wrote just before Frost returned to the United States from England. Therefore, when Pound was tried for treasonous broadcasts made in Rome during World War II, Frost was not surprised. To him, the man's behavior was only one more example of Pound's abrasive tendencies.

Then on July 4, 1954, a review of Ezra Pound's book, *The Literary Essays of Ezra Pound,* appeared in *The New York Times Book Review*. The writer quoted from that book a 1914 review by Pound of Frost's *North of Boston*. Frost had never before seen that review. In it Pound declared, "Mr. Frost is an honest writer, writing from himself, from his own knowledge and emotion. . . . [Frost] has given [the New England people's] life honestly and seriously. . . . I know more of farm life than I did before I had read his poems. That means I know more of life."

Now, Frost was willing to change his attitude and consider whether Pound's lifetime sentence was justified if he was still insane and could not be tried. In 1957, when MacLeish asked Frost to sign a letter to President Eisenhower requesting Pound's release, he agreed.

The letter, signed also by T. S. Eliot and Ernest Hemingway, requested a review of Pound's case. Shortly thereafter, the three men received an invitation to come to Washington to discuss the case with the assistant attorney general. Frost did not reply to the request because, at the time, he was making plans for a trip to England as a goodwill ambassador. Pressured by MacLeish, Frost agreed to a meeting after he returned to the United States. The first meeting occurred in July, but the government still had reservations because of Pound's association with some segregationists. Once Frost became involved, he went all out and returned to Washington by himself in October. This time he asked for Pound's transfer to a private facility if the government would not release Pound.

Nothing happened for the next couple of months. Then Frost received the Poetry Society's Gold Medal along with a telegram of congratulations from President Eisenhower. Suddenly Frost saw a way that he might help Pound. He began to work for a personal meeting with the president. In February, he received a letter from Eisenhower inviting him to a stag dinner at the White House on the twenty-seventh. Frost also managed to secure a luncheon engagement with the U.S. attorney general the day before the dinner. Pound's freedom became a possibility and, ultimately, a reality on April 18, 1958, when the government dismissed all charges. When newspapers headlined Pound's release, most credited Frost with having brought it about, despite the fact that MacLeish spearheaded the effort. However, Pound showed no particular gratitude for Frost's work on his behalf. When told what Frost had done, Pound, who had been held for eleven years, remarked, "He ain't been in much of a hurry." However, when a friend called Pound's attention to an editorial that said Frost had repaid Pound for his help in England, Pound replied, "Frost's debt was paid when he published *North of Boston.*"

In October 1958, Frost began work as a poetry consultant at the Library of Congress. Like many of his other recent positions, the job entailed few responsibilities. Basically, he had to build up the poetry collection, arrange for poetry readings, answer questions from the public, and serve as the national poetry figurehead. Frost worked so hard in this position, though, that he later became honorary Consultant for the Humanities. His cultural work led to his being awarded a $2,500 Congressional Medal "in recognition of his poetry, which has enriched the culture of the United States and the philosophy of the world."

On March 26, 1959, publisher Henry Holt and Company celebrated Frost's eighty-fifth birthday with another dinner at the Waldorf-Astoria Hotel in New York. The featured speaker for the occasion was Lionel Trilling, a noted American critic. In his remarks about Frost, Trilling shocked the audience by saying, "I think of Robert Frost as a terrifying poet. Call him, if it makes things any easier, a tragic poet." He compared Frost's works to *Studies in Classic American Literature* by D. H. Lawrence to show that American writers had rid themselves of old beliefs to represent instead "the terrible actualities of life in a new way."

Trilling's remarks resembled Randall Jarrell's earlier comments about Frost's dark side, to Frost's displeasure. For some reason, Frost was especially nervous that night and may have had difficulty in hearing all that Trilling said. He heard the comparison to Lawrence and did not like it. When Frost rose to speak, his response was halting and uncertain. He stumbled and even forgot lines to some of his own poems. He asked the audience if they found him terrifying.

Trilling intended the comment as praise for the depth and power of Frost's work. What he meant was that Frost's poetry was not limited to pastoral scenes. Trilling tried to show that poems dealing with loneliness, fear of the world's destruction, and the soul's emptiness all pointed to a poet who understood the grim realities of the twentieth century. If nothing else, Trilling's remarks caused people to take a new look at Frost's poetry. In a later exchange of letters, Trilling and Frost indicated no hard feelings on either side.

After his famous reading at President Kennedy's inauguration, Frost returned to Vermont with the kind of notoriety only television could deliver, intent on finishing his last book of poems. At eighty-seven years old, he worried that the poems might not be good and hesitated to release them. The volume contained forty poems from different stages of Frost's life and represented most of his stylistic features: joyful lyrics, sonnets, ironic humor, satire, metaphysical connections, symbols and metaphors. His topics ranged from nature to the American character to outer space. Frost saw this volume as his last chance to tell "all that he thought was true."

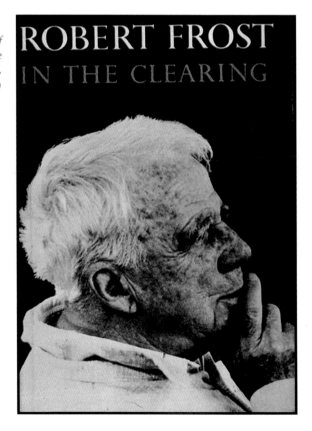

The cover of the trade edition of Frost's last collection, In the Clearing, *published March 26, 1962.* (University of Virginia)

ROBERT FROST
IN THE CLEARING

Published on his eighty-eighth birthday, *In the Clearing* became an instant best-seller and eventually sold 100,000 copies. Critics, mostly Frost's friends, wrote positive reviews, several commenting about the way the poems reflected both a poet of passion and one with wit and whimsy. In his poem "It Takes All Sorts," Frost recognizes this duality within himself:

> It takes all sorts of in- and outdoor schooling
> To get adapted to my kind of fooling.

Frost went back to Washington in May in connection with his duties as consultant in the humanities. While he was there, Stewart Udall, secretary of the interior in the Kennedy administration, asked Frost if he would like to go to Russia as part of a cultural exchange. Frost hesitated because of his health and age. He decided that he would go only if extended a personal invitation by President Kennedy. His other stipulation was that he wanted to meet Nikita Khrushchev.

Kennedy did extend the invite. With no assurance that he would get to meet the Soviet leader, Frost left for Russia accompanied by Udall and several others. In the Soviet Union, Frost spent the days in lectures and interviews. At night he dined with some of Russia's best writers. Wherever he went, the people responded to him warmly. However, Russian officials believed that there was a negative reference to the Berlin Wall in the first line of Frost's poem "Mending Wall." When a translator read the poem, he omitted the first line: "Something there is that doesn't love a wall."

Frost still wanted to speak to Khrushchev. He grew so anxious about the meeting that when the invitation finally came, he developed severe stomach cramps. The Soviet leader agreed to meet with Frost because he saw Frost as Kennedy's ambassador. Khrushchev hoped that Frost would believe Russia's leader to be a decent, capable leader and that Frost would carry that impression back to the president.

Because of Frost's illness, Khrushchev came to Frost's room. They discussed a broad array of topics: the danger of nuclear war, economic conflict between the United

Frost and Nikita Khrushchev (far right) *meet during Frost's visit to the Soviet Union in 1962.* (Courtesy of Dartmouth College Library.)

States and the Soviet Union, and American and Russian cultural traditions. Frost then began a rather rambling acknowledgement of the conflict between the United States and the Soviet Union. Secretary Udall later reported that Frost told the Soviet premier "that there should be no petty squabbles, that there must be a noble rivalry between Russia and the United States, forcefully and magnanimously pressed by the leaders of both sides." Frost believed that such a relationship would mean the end of propaganda and name-calling and would result in a recognition of each other's greatness and power. Even after this statement, Khrushchev sensed that Frost was holding back and asked him directly if he had something special on his mind. Frost admitted he did and got to the real issue—the separation of Berlin by the wall.

When Germany surrendered at the end of World War II, the victorious Allies divided the capital city between East (under Soviet control) and West (initially occupied by the United States, Britain, and other Allies) in 1961. A towering concrete wall physically separated the two sides and it came to represent the political divide between the capitalist, democratic West and the Communist countries of Eastern Europe.

Frost suggested to Khrushchev that the city be reunited. The two discussed the issue for an hour and a half with neither yielding his position. Finally, Khrushchev rose, shook hands, conveyed greetings to Kennedy and left. As Khrushchev departed, Frost said, "He's a great man. He knows what power is and isn't afraid to take hold of it. He's a great man, all right." Though Frost did not agree with the Soviet Union's position on many issues, he respected the man who led that nation. What Frost did not see was the cold, cruel side of Khrushchev, who six weeks later put the world on the brink of disaster when he placed nuclear weapons in Cuba.

Frost flew home September 9. Exhausted after a seventeen-hour flight, he tried to avoid reporters. When they persisted, Frost made some impromptu remarks about his meeting with Khrushchev. He came to regret those remarks, as he often did when he spoke before thinking. Frost told the reporters that Khrushchev had said the United States was "too liberal to fight." For years Frost had criticized liberals as hesitant, overcautious types who avoided the realities of power. He could not resist an opportunity to tease them but quickly understood what a mistake he had made in giving in to the urge.

The remark caused a stir, and some people wondered if Frost was trying to provoke trouble between the United States and Russia. Though President Kennedy's aides assured him that the remark sounded more like Frost than Khrushchev, the president never contacted Frost to thank him for going to the Soviet Union, and the greetings from Khrushchev to Kennedy were never delivered. Frost soon realized that there was a difference between joking on the lecture circuit and joking about international relationships.

Age was taking its toll on Frost, and his health suffered. Doctors warned him that he needed prostate surgery soon. In typical fashion, though, Frost kept going. When he went to Amherst for the fall, he learned that the college had received a $3.5 million donation to construct the Robert Frost Library. On October 23, Frost went to Washington, DC, to address the National Poetry Festival at the Library of Congress. Tension filled the city as President Kennedy dealt with the Cuban missile crisis and averted a nuclear war. Some claimed that Frost's offhand comment about the United States not being willing to fight strengthened Kennedy's resolve in the incident.

However, in his address to the Library of Congress, Frost corrected that misunderstanding. He confessed that Khrushchev had not said that the United States was too liberal to fight. What he had said was "There's such a thing as a nation getting so soft it couldn't—wouldn't fight." Frost further explained that Khrushchev did not make the remark about the United States in particular.

Although Frost made several other lecture presentations, an urgent need for prostate surgery interrupted his schedule. In his last interview before going to the hospital, Frost told reporters: "I don't take life very seriously. It's hard to get into this world and hard to get out of it. And what's in between doesn't make much sense. If that sounds pessimistic, let it stand."

In addition to the prostate condition, tests revealed an infected bladder and a weak, irregular heartbeat.

U.S. 10¢

Robert Frost

AMERICAN POET

This American postage stamp was issued on March 26, 1974, honoring Robert Frost on the centennial of his birth. (United States Postal Service)

When a stoppage in the bladder occurred, doctors performed immediate surgery. Unfortunately, the surgery revealed that the prostate was malignant and that the cancer had spread to the bladder. Amazingly, Frost recovered from the surgery but almost died from a blood clot in his lungs on December 23. In addition, his heart showed damage. On January 7, he had another blood clot in his lungs.

Although Kay Morrison tried to limit his visitors, they came in a steady procession. One who was always welcome was Louis Untermeyer. However, he had the unpleasant duty of telling Frost that John Steinbeck had won the 1962 Nobel Prize for Literature, killing any hope that Frost would ever win that award.

Near midnight on January 28, 1963, Frost lost consciousness and died in the early morning hours from another pulmonary embolism. A seventy-two-year career in writing poetry came to an end, just two months away from Frost's eighty-ninth birthday.

On January 30, Frost's body was cremated at the Mount Auburn Cemetery and later buried in the Old Cemetery in Bennington at the Old First Congregational Church, where Frost had earlier purchased plots for his entire family. According to his will, Kay Morrison received more property and cash than all of Frost's living children and his daughter-in-law combined.

For all the generations that have read, memorized, and cherished the poems of Robert Frost, he certainly accomplished his goal "to lodge a few pebbles. . . ." With his strong belief in self-reliance, Frost's poems rarely suggested any feeling of brotherhood. He believed that each man must stand alone—responsible for himself and his family. No other poet knew the New England countryside and its inhabitants like Frost, and he left readers everywhere a legacy of poems about the struggling lives of stoic New Englanders.

Through his ability to use language in a special way, he communicated a vision of the human experience. Frost recognized experience as a continually changing process that constantly opened new options and fresh choices. In response to those who saw him as only a pastoral poet, he contended, "Some people have called me a nature poet, because of the background, but I'm not a nature poet. There's always something else in my poetry." It is this "something else" that lodged itself in the hearts and imaginations of his readers.

Although he never won the Nobel Prize for Literature, the world's accolade for its best writers, Robert Frost's work is ultimately ranked with those who have. His "sound of sense," colloquial diction, and intricate poetic constructions influenced many other poets, such as Edward Thomas, Robert Graves, W. H. Auden, James Dickey, Donald Hall, Richard Wilbur, and Theodore Roethke. Many British readers saw Frost as the American counterpart to their poets William Wordsworth and Alfred Lord Tennyson.

President John F. Kennedy paid final tribute to Frost when he spoke at the dedication of the Robert Frost

Library at Amherst College on October 26, 1963:

This day, devoted to the memory of Robert Frost, offers an opportunity for reflection which is prized by politicians as well as by others and even by poets. For Robert Frost was one of the granite figures of our time in America. He was supremely two things—an artist and an American. . . .

In honoring Robert Frost we therefore can pay honor to the deepest sources of our national strength. That strength takes many forms and the most obvious forms are not always the most significant. . . .

He brought an unsparing instinct for reality to bear on the platitudes and pieties of society. His sense of the human tragedy fortified him against self-deception and easy consolation.

. . . because he knew the midnight as well as the high noon, because he understood the ordeal as well as the triumph of the human spirit, he gave his age strength with which to overcome despair.

Timeline

1874	Robert Lee Frost born in San Francisco, California, on March 26.
1885	Father dies.
1892	Frost graduates from Lawrence High School; enrolls as freshman at Dartmouth College in Hanover, New Hampshire; leaves Dartmouth in December.
1894	Sells his first poem, "My Butterfly: An Elegy."
1895	Marries Elinor Miriam White on December 19.
1896	Son Elliott is born on September 25.
1897	Attends Harvard University as a special student.
1899	Withdraws from Harvard in March; daughter Lesley born on April 28; borrows money from grandfather to start poultry farm.
1900	Son Elliott dies at age 4 in July; mother enters sanitarium and dies of cancer on November 2.
1901	Grandfather dies in July, leaving Frost an annuity and use of Derry farm for ten years.
1902	Son Carol born on May 27.
1903	Daughter Irma born on June 27.
1905	Daughter Marjorie born on March 29.
1906	Begins teaching at Pinkerton Academy, Derry, New Hampshire.

1907	Daughter Elinor Bettina born on June 18; dies three days later.
1911	Accepts teaching position at New Hampshire State Normal School; sells Derry farm.
1912	In August, Frost and family sail for England.
1913	David Nutt and Company of London publishes *A Boy's Will*.
1914	Family moves to Gloucestershire in April; World War I begins; *North of Boston* published by David Nutt; New York publisher Henry Holt and Company secures American rights to Frost's books of poetry.
1915	Frost family returns to United States in February and settles on a farm near Franconia, New Hampshire.
1916	Begins lecture and reading tours; *Mountain Interval* published in November.
1917	Joins Amherst College faculty as professor of English.
1920	Resigns from Amherst; aids in founding Bread Loaf School of English.
1923	Publishes *New Hampshire* and *Selected Poems*; enters new two-year contract with Amherst.
1924	Accepts University of Michigan fellowship to begin in fall of 1925; receives Pulitzer Prize for *New Hampshire*.
1926	Returns to Amherst as Professor of English.
1928	Publishes *West-Running Brook*.
1929	Sister Jeanie dies at age fifty-three in a sanatorium.
1930	Elected to American Academy of Arts and Letters.
1931	Awarded Pulitzer Prize for *Collected Poems*.
1934	Daughter Marjorie dies on May 2.
1936	Delivers Charles Eliot Norton lectures at Harvard University; *A Further Range* is published in June.
1937	Receives third Pulitzer Prize for *A Further Range*.
1938	Elinor Frost dies in Florida on March 20; Frost resigns from Amherst.

1939	Receives Gold Medal from National Institute of Arts; accepts position as Ralph Waldo Emerson Fellow in Poetry at Harvard.
1940	Son Carol commits suicide on October 9.
1941	Frost's work exhibited at Library of Congress; accepts position as Fellow of American Civilization at Harvard.
1942	Publishes *A Witness Tree.*
1943	Wins Pulitzer Prize for *A Witness Tree*; begins position as George Ticknor Fellow in the Humanities at Dartmouth.
1945	Publishes *A Masque of Reason.*
1947	Publishes *Steeple Bush* and *A Masque of Mercy.*
1948	Amherst College confers honorary doctor of letters degree on Frost.
1949	Goes back to Amherst as Simpson Lecturer in Literature; publishes *The Complete Poems of Robert Frost.*
1950	United States Senate honors Frost with resolution on his seventy-fifth birthday.
1953	Wins $5,000 Academy of American Poets award.
1954	Publisher Henry Holt and Company honors Frost with dinner on eightieth birthday; Frost serves as delegate to World Conference of Writers in Sao Paulo, Brazil.
1958	Serves as Consultant in Poetry for Library of Congress; receives $2,500 Congressional Medal.
1959	Holt celebrates Frost's eighty-fifth birthday with New York dinner; Frost appointed to three-year term as Honorary Consultant in the Humanities for Library of Congress.
1961	Reads "The Gift Outright" at John F. Kennedy's inauguration.
1962	Publishes last book of poems, *In the Clearing*, on eighty-eighth birthday; travels to Soviet Union as part of cultural exchange and meets with Nikita Khrushchev;

anonymous person donates $3.5 million to Amherst for Robert Frost Library; addresses National Poetry Festival at Library of Congress during time of Cuban missile crisis; enters hospital for prostate surgery. 1963 Awarded $2,500 Bollingen Prize for *In the Clearing;* dies in Boston at age eighty-eight; Frost's body cremated and later interred in Old Bennington Cemetery, Vermont.

Sources

CHAPTER ONE: Seeds of a Poet's Life

p. 12, "You know that Frost . . ." Lawrance Thompson and R. H. Winnick, *Robert Frost: The Later Years, 1938-1963* (New York: Holt, Rinehart and Winston, 1976), 277.

p. 12-13, "I'm not having . . ." Jeffrey Meyers, *Robert Frost: A Biography* (Boston: Houghton Mifflin Company, 1996), 323.

p. 14, "Such as she . . ." Jay Parini, *Robert Frost: A Life* (New York: Henry Holt and Company, 1999), 414.

p. 24, "All this baptizing . . ." Meyers, *Robert Frost: A Biography*, 10.

p. 25, "I never spoke . . ." Elizabeth Shepley Sergeant, *Robert Frost: The Trial by Existence* (New York: Holt, Rinehart and Winston, 1976), 15.

p. 26, "the *longest, loneliest* . . ." Parini, *Robert Frost: A Life*, 19.

CHAPTER TWO: "The Self Seeker"

p. 31, "You wait. Some day . . ." Lawrance Thompson, *Robert Frost: The Early Years, 1874-1915* (New York: Holt, Rinehart and Winston, 1966), 77.

p. 32, "In a word, our . . ." Ibid., 91.

p. 33, "I had never written . . ." Meyers, *Robert Frost: A Biography*, 19.

p. 33, "No one would think . . ." Thompson, *The Early Years*, 112.

p. 36, "I was glad . . ." Parini, *Robert Frost: A Life*, 37.

p. 38, "Word I was . . ." Edward Connery Lathem, ed., *The Poetry of Robert Frost* (New York: Holt, Rinehart and Winston, 1969), 251.

p. 41, "a momentary stay . . ." Parini, *Robert Frost: A Life*, 42.

p. 42, "I'm sure the old . . ." Ibid., 46.

p. 44, "I often think . . ." Ibid., 49.

p. 44, "I suppose it was . . ." Meyers, *Robert Frost: A Biography*, 33.

CHAPTER THREE: A Poet's Will

p. 47, "They could not . . ." Parini, *Robert Frost: A Life*, 64.

p. 48-49, "This is *cholera* . . ." Thompson, *The Early Years*, 258.

p. 50, "It all started . . ." Parini, *Robert Frost: A Life*, 72.

p. 52, "Take your choice . . ." Meyers, *Robert Frost: A Biography*, 60.

p. 52, "to do what I hated . . ." Ibid., 63.

p. 55, "The coin chose . . ." Thompson, *The Early Years*, 390.

p. 57, "My mother never worked . . ." John Evangelist Walsh, *Into My Own: The English Years of Robert Frost 1912-1915* (New York: Grove Weidenfeld, 1988), 22.

p. 57, "I wasn't going . . ." Ibid., 32.

p. 58, "A boy's will . . ." Henry Wadsworth Longfellow, American Poems, http://www.americanpoems.com/poets/longfellow/19230 (accessed December 19, 2005).

p. 58, "comes pretty near . . ." Parini, *Robert Frost: A Life,* 119.

p. 58, "a series of lyrics . . ." Meyers, *Robert Frost: A Biography*, 100.

p. 58, "they wist . . ." Lathem, *The Poetry of Robert Frost*, 15.

p. 58, "that frighted thee . . ." Ibid., 28.

p. 59, "We [the children] were . . ." Parini, *Robert Frost: A Life*, 122.

CHAPTER FOUR: England's Literary World

p. 62, "At home . . ." Walsh, *Into My Own,* 89.

p. 62, "the best poetry . . ." Ibid., 96.

p. 64, "I had as soon . . ." Robert C. Petersen, ed., *Robert Frost: A Collection of Poems* (Boston: Wadsworth, 2004), 38.

p. 65, "There is an agreeable . . ." Thompson, *The Early Years*, 414-415.

p. 66, "One feels that . . ." "Procession of the Muses," in *Robert Frost: The Critical Perception*, edited by Linda W. Wagner (New York: Burt Franklin & Co., Inc., 1977), 5.

p. 66, "My dream would be . . ." Walsh, *Into My Own,* 149.

p. 69, "Out walking in the . . ." Lathem, *The Poetry of Robert Frost*, 101.

p. 71, "To warm the . . ." Ibid., 102.

p. 71, "a sentence *must* . . ." Lawrance Thompson, ed., *Selected Letters of Robert Frost* (New York: Holt, Rinehart and Winston, 1964), 204.

p. 72, " 'Home,' he mocked . . ." Lathem, *The Poetry of Robert Frost*, 38.

p. 72, "Poetry burns up . . ." Thompson, *The Early Years*, 451.

p. 72, "Poetry, in this book . . ." Walsh, *Into My Own,* 172.

p. 73, "Now we can go . . ." Ibid., 205.

CHAPTER FIVE: Unknown at Home

p. 75, "the most American . . ." Lawrance Thompson, *Robert Frost: The Years of Triumph, 1915-1938* (New York: Holt, Rinehart, and Winston, 1970), 3.

p. 82, "I shall be telling . . ." Lathem, *The Poetry of Robert Frost*, 105.

p. 82, "sincerity in perception . . ." Sidney Cox, "The Sincerity of Robert Frost," in *Robert Frost: The Critical Reception*, edited by Linda W. Wagner (New York: Burt Franklin & Co., Inc., 1977), 47.

p. 83, "I should awfully . . ." Meyers, *Robert Frost: A Biography*, 151.

p. 83, "Edward Thomas was . . ." Thompson, *The Years of Triumph*, 94.

p. 86, "I've kicked myself . . ." Parini, *Robert Frost: A Life*, 193.

p. 87-88, "My hope is . . ." Thompson, *The Years of Triumph*, 124.

p. 91, "A poem is an idea . . ." Reginald L. Cook, *The Dimensions of Robert Frost* (New York: Rinehart & Company, Inc., 1958), 76.

p. 91, "cutting across one another . . ." Ibid., 60.

p. 92, "The woods are lovely . . ." Lathem, *The Poetry of Robert Frost*, 224-225.

p. 95, "Nature's first green . . ." Ibid., 222-223.

CHAPTER SIX: "The Door in the Dark"

p. 96-97, "A born teacher . . ." Philip L. Gerber, *Robert Frost* (Boston: Twayne Publishers, 1982), 15.

p. 97, "I always dreamed . . ." Parini, *Robert Frost: A Life*, 227.

p. 100, "Your father *must* give . . ." Meyers, *Robert Frost: A Biography*, 187.

p. 100, "I never write about . . ." Parini, *Robert Frost: A Life*, 236.

p. 101, "Frost began to discuss . . ." Ibid., 243.

p. 104-105, "His verse . . ." Meyers, *Robert Frost: A Biography*, 199.

p. 105, "I will if Frost . . ." Sergeant, *Robert Frost: The Trial by Existence*, 314.

p. 106, "The noblest of us . . ." Louis Untermeyer, *The Letters of Robert Frost to Louis Untermeyer* (New York: Holt, Rinehart and Winston, 1963), 241.

p. 107, "It may come to . . ." Parini, *Robert Frost: A Life*, 296.

p. 109, "Die early and avoid . . ." Lathem, *The Poetry of Robert Frost*, 317.

p. 110, "the importance of poetry . . ." Parini, *Robert Frost: A Life*, 304.

p. 111-112, "The voice is still . . ." Ibid., 306.

p. 112, "Mr. Frost now occupies . . ." Meyers, *Robert Frost: A Biography*, 220.

p. 113, "I'm afraid I dragged . . ." Ibid., 231.

p. 114, "I shall be all . . ." Thompson, *The Years of Triumph*, 501.

CHAPTER SEVEN: A Man with Friends

p. 117, "You two rescued . . ." Thompson and Winnick, *The Later Years*, 13.

p. 120, "it begins in delight . . ." Ibid., 31.

p. 120, "distinguished work . . ." Parini, *Robert Frost: A Life*, 325.

p. 124, "Disaster brought out . . ." Meyers, *Robert Frost: A Biography*, 277.

p. 124-125, "I took the wrong . . ." Untermeyer, *The Letters of Robert Frost*, 322-323.

CHAPTER EIGHT: Poet-in-Residence

p. 127-128, "democracy would always . . ." Thompson and Winnick, *The Later Years*, 78.

p. 128, "The land was ours . . ." Lathem, *The Poetry of Robert Frost*, 348.

p. 129, "There was never . . ." Parini, *Robert Frost: A Life*, 338.

p. 130-131, "There is much in . . ." Lathem, *The Poetry of Robert Frost*, 349.

p. 131, "His writing is clearer . . ." Adam Margoshes, "Robert Frost, Semi-Poet," in *Robert Frost: The Critical Reception*, edited by Linda W. Wagner (New York: Burt Franklin & Co.,

Inc., 1977), 175.

p. 131, "This is a beautiful . . ." Stephen Vincent Benet, "Frost at Sixty-Seven," in *Robert Frost: The Critical Reception*, edited by Linda W. Wagner (New York: Burt Franklin & Co., Inc., 1977), 169.

p. 134, "Frost, bringing us . . ." Meyers, *Robert Frost: A Biography*, 280.

p. 134, "a bad book . . ." Ibid., 281.

p. 136, "Most of the poems . . ." Randall Jarrell, "Tenderness and Passive Sadness," in *Robert Frost: The Critical Reception*, edited by Linda W. Wagner (New York: Burt Franklin & Co., Inc., 1977), 209.

p. 137, "begin with a flat . . ." Ibid., 318.

p. 137, "subtlest and saddest . . ." Ibid., 209.

p. 138, "Cast your eye . . ." Untermeyer, *The Letters of Robert Frost*, 346.

CHAPTER NINE: Quilt of Honors

p. 141, "Of living U.S. poets . . ." Parini, *Robert Frost: A Life*, 381.

p. 141, "to lodge a few . . ." John Doyle, Jr., *The Poetry of Robert Frost: An Analysis* (New York: Hafner Press, 1962), 263.

p. 143, "the sale of the collection. . ." Thomas and Winnick, *The Later Years*, 192.

p. 143, "reportedly the highest. . ." Parini, *Robert Frost: A Life*, 378.

p. 144-145, "Mr. Frost is an honest . . ." Thompson and Winnick, *The Later Years*, 248.

p. 146, "He ain't been . . ." Parini, *Robert Frost: A Life*, 405.

p. 146, "Frost's debt was paid . . ." Meyers, *Robert Frost: A Biography*, 315.

p. 146, "in recognition of . . ." Thompson and Winnick, *The Later Years*, 276.

p. 147, "I think of Robert Frost . . ." Meyers, *Robert Frost: A Biography*, 318.

p. 147, "the terrible actualities . . ." William H. Pritchard, *Frost: A Literary Life Reconsidered* (New York: Oxford University Press, 1984), 252.

p. 148, "all that he thought . . ." Elizabeth Isaacs, *An Introduction to Robert Frost* (Denver: Allen Swallow, 1962), 85.

p. 149, "It takes all sorts . . ." Lathem, *The Poetry of Robert Frost*, 470.

p. 150, "Something there is . . ." Ibid., 33.

p. 151, "that there should be . . ." Pritchard, *Frost: A Literary Life Reconsidered*, 253.

p. 151-152, "He's a great man . . ." Parini, *Robert Frost: A Life*, 434.

p. 152, "too liberal . . ." Thompson and Winnick, *The Later Years*, 323.

p. 153, "There's such a thing . . ." Ibid., 328.

p. 153, "I don't take life . . ." Meyers, *Robert Frost: A Biography*, 346.

p. 155, "to lodge a few . . ." John Doyle, Jr., *The Poetry of Robert Frost: An Analysis* (New York: Hafner Press, 1962), 263.

p. 156, "Some people have . . ." Reginald L. Cook, *Robert Frost: A Living Voice* (Amherst: The University of Massachusetts Press, 1974), 308.

p. 157, "This day, devoted to . . ." Thompson and Winnick, *The Later Years*, 347-48.

Bibliography

Cook, Reginald L. *The Dimensions of Robert Frost*. New York: Rinehart & Company, Inc., 1958.

———. *Robert Frost: A Living Voice*. Amherst: The University of Massachusetts Press, 1974.

Doyle, John, Jr. *The Poetry of Robert Frost: An Analysis*. New York: Hafner Press, 1962.

Gerber, Philip L. *Robert Frost*. Boston: Twayne Publishers, 1982.

Isaacs, Elizabeth. *An Introduction to Robert Frost*. Denver, CO: Allen Swallow, 1962.

Lathem, Edward Connery, ed. *The Poetry of Robert Frost*. New York: Holt, Rinehart and Winston, 1969.

Meyers, Jeffrey. *Robert Frost: A Biography*. Boston: Houghton Mifflin Company, 1996.

Parini, Jay. "The Art of Reading Robert Frost." Poets & Writers Magazine Online. http://www.pw.org/mag/parini3.htm.

———. *Robert Frost: A Life*. New York: Henry Holt and Company, 1999.

Petersen, Robert C., ed. *Robert Frost: A Collection of Poems*. Boston: Wadsworth, 2004.

Pritchard, William H. *Frost: A Literary Life Reconsidered*. New York: Oxford University Press, 1984.

Sergeant, Elizabeth Shepley. *The Trial by Existence*. New York: Holt, Rinehart, and Winston, 1976.

Thompson, Lawrance. *Robert Frost: The Early Years, 1874-1915*. New York: Holt, Rinehart and Winston, 1966.

————. *Robert Frost: The Years of Triumph, 1915-1938*. New York: Holt, Rinehart and Winston, 1970.

————. ed. *Selected Letters of Robert Frost*. New York: Holt, Rinehart and Winston, 1964.

Thompson, Lawrance and R. H. Winnick. *Robert Frost: The Later Years, 1938-1963*. New York: Holt, Rinehart and Winston, 1976.

Untermeyer, Louis. *The Letters of Robert Frost to Louis Untermeyer*. New York: Holt, Rinehart and Winston, 1963.

Wagner, Linda W., ed. *Robert Frost: The Critical Reception*. New York: Burt Franklin & Co., Inc., 1977.

Walsh, John Evangelist. *Into My Own: The English Years of Robert Frost*. New York: Grove Weidenfeld, 1988.

Web sites

http://www.ketzle.com/frost/
This Web site dedicated to Robert Frost features dozens of Frost's poems, a short biography, and links to other sites of interest to Frost fans.

http://www.frostfriends.org
This Web site, sponsored by the Friends of Robert Frost, for the Robert Frost Stone House Museum includes a Robert Frost tutorial, library, newsletters, biography, and a chronology.

http://www.americaslibrary.gov/cgi-bin/page.cgi/jb/modern/ frost_1
A copied image of the actual manuscripts from which Frost read his dedication and "The Gift Outright."

http://www.poets.org/
The Academy of American Poets sponsors National Poetry Month in April, publishes *American Poet* magazine, and sponsors awards and a host of other programs supporting the writing and reading of poetry. The site maintains an inventory of poems available for reading online and histories of some of the country's most famous poets.

http://www.pulitzer.org/
In 1917, Joseph Pulitzer established the Pulitzer Prize awards to recognize excellence in journalism and literature. The site includes the history of the award, a list of winners since its inception, and other resources.

http://www.swedenborg.org/
This church community, started in the late eighteenth century, was founded under the teachings of Swedish scientist and theologian Emanuel Swedenborg. Today, there are approximately 2,600 followers in the United States and 50,000 worldwide. The Web site details the religion's history and beliefs.

Index